AR DENIAL?

Healing a Heart that is Hurt

Copyright © 2023
Dr. Paulina A. Cole-Hardy

All rights reserved. This book or any portion thereof may not be reproduced or used in any manner whatsoever without the express written permission of the publisher except for the use of brief quotations in a book review.

The Bible verses used came from the King James version.

Printed in the United States of America
First printing, 2023

ARE YOU IN DENIAL?
Dr. Cole-Hardy

TABLE OF CONTENTS

Chapter 1:

Facing the Truth

The Denial Dilemma

Recognizing the Repeating Patterns

The Quest for Lasting Love

Chapter 2:

The Common Thread

Love Knows No Boundaries

Attracting the Same Types

Breaking Down Stereotypes

Chapter 3:

The Fear of Loneliness

The Loneliness Paradox

Overcoming the Fear

Embracing Solitude

Chapter 4:
Unmasking Your Desires
Defining Your Ideal Partner
Differentiating Between Wants and Needs
Seeking God's Will in Your Desires

Chapter 5:
Self-Love and Self-Worth
Understanding Self-Love
Discovering Your Worth in Christ
Building a Foundation of Self-Respect

Chapter 6:
Breaking the Cycle
Identifying Negative Patterns
Choosing Different Paths
The Power of Self-Reflection

Chapter 7:
Trusting God's Timing
Surrendering Control
Patience in the Waiting
Faith in God's Plan

Chapter 8:
Strengthening Your Faith
The Role of Faith in Relationships
Praying for Clarity and Guidance
Cultivating a Spiritual Connection

Chapter 9:
Building Healthy Relationships
Setting Boundaries
Effective Communication
Growing Together in Christ

Chapter 10:
Embracing Your Singleness
The Beauty of Singleness
Serving God Wholeheartedly
Preparing for the Right One

Conclusion:
Breaking Free from Denial

INTRODUCTION

There is a ubiquitous pattern in a world full of various experiences that cuts across both faith and culture. Untold numbers of women, both Christian and non-Christian, become caught up in this pattern. They wrestle with a straightforward yet important question: "Are you in denial?" It reverberates throughout the peaceful moments of their life.

These ladies, who come from all different origins and areas of life, appear to be drawn to guys who assume different personas and disguises. These men may have diverse looks on the outside due to their status, sizes, shapes, and colors, but they all have disappointment as a common emotion. These ladies are left feeling lost in a sea of sadness by the pattern that appears with a terrifying regularity, a story of repeated blunders.

Imagine this: Sarah is a devoted Christian who has a heart full of optimism but also experiences heartbreak more often than she cares to confess. She has encountered guys from diverse areas of life, each of whom gave her a different sense of hope but ultimately left her feeling disappointed. Mary, a non-Christian friend of hers, who finds herself in a startlingly similar situation while holding different beliefs, can relate to the story.

Although Sarah and Mary's stories may appear unusual, they are only two of the many women who have been caught in this vicious circle. Then the question: Why do they keep doing the same thing wrong? The solution is partially found in the grasp of fear, specifically the fear of being alone and having to deal with the solitude and silence that might come along with it.

But I'll take you on a tour across these pages that aims to make sense of this bewildering pattern. We examine the intricate nature of attraction, analyze the draw of familiarity, and consider the weighty load of previous disappointments. This path does not include passing judgment but rather understanding since it acknowledges the vulnerability of the human heart and the desire for connection that exists in every one of us.

We will come across tales of resiliency, self-discovery, and instances of unshakeable faith as we navigate the difficulties of these women's lives. We will investigate the impact of altering our viewpoints and expectations to ultimately liberate ourselves from self-doubt and denial.

Consequently, this book is your invitation to join us on a transforming journey if you've ever wondered if you might be caught in the web of denial if you've ever tasted the harsh sting of heartache on repeat, or if you've ever sensed the towering shadow of loneliness. Together, we will discover the knowledge, conviction, and bravery required to break free from ingrained habits and courageously enter a new phase of life, one marked by hope, purpose, and the real promise of love.

CHAPTER 1

FACING THE TRUTH

Philippians 3:13-14   Isaiah 43:18-19

In the narrative of our lives, we frequently find ourselves at a fork in the road where the present and the past clash with the unstoppable force of reality. We have all traveled this trip in our unique ways, therefore it is a universal journey that cuts through age, gender, and experience barriers. No matter how many heartbreaks you've experienced, the path is defined by one straightforward yet significant instruction: face reality and go forward.

The truth frequently shows up after relationships have fallen apart, like an unexpected guest whose presence cannot be denied. The stark reality necessitates awareness, a coming to terms with the decisions taken and the results experienced. However, many of us are reluctant to take this journey due to our concern about the potential pain. But, as human beings, we are inherently resilient. We possess an innate capacity to confront our innermost fears, our past mistakes, and the broken pieces of our hearts. In doing so, we unlock a transformative power that leads us down a path of healing, self-discovery, and growth. So, let's explore this fascinating topic together, dear reader. As we travel the complex terrain of our emotions and experiences, let us simply explain the importance of facing the truth. No matter how many times you've experienced the agonizing path of heartbreak, keep in mind that facing the truth is a courageous step toward a better, more genuine future rather than an admission of defeat.

We frequently discover ourselves trapped in regret, hatred, and grief that are spun from the ruins of a relationship, a job, or a dream that once contained our hearts in its intricate connection to life. It's a feeling that is as universal as the human condition itself because none of us are exempt from the hardships that life may bring us. However, one fundamental fact emerges despite the devastation of these setbacks: we cannot afford to stay in the shadows of the past; we must move forward.

Think about Sarah, a lady who invested her heart and soul into a union that split apart due to unfulfilled expectations and broken promises. Her world fell apart, leaving a broken mosaic of suffering and disappointment. Or consider James, who invested years in a career that ultimately made him feel confined and unhappy. He could feel the oppressive shackles of sorrow squeezing him every morning as he dragged himself to work. Many of us may relate to these stories. The hard reality of unmet expectations and the torture of what-ifs may have faced Sarah or James at some point in their life. At this point, we must decide whether to keep sinking deeper into despair or muster the will to go forward.

We have a remarkable ability for resilience as humans. It's a characteristic that enables us to face our most significant wounds and accept the lessons they contain. We discover a wellspring of possibility, a route to healing, and the chance to create a future that differs from our past when we face the reality of our circumstances. So, let's start this transformational adventure together, dear reader. Let's examine the great wisdom of confronting the truth as an act of bravery and self-empowerment rather than as a capitulation. No matter how many times life has put us to the test, we must never forget that our power comes from our capacity to break free from the bonds of the past and go on, creating a new story that is rich with resilience, hope, and purpose.

Philippians 3:13-14 "Brethren, I count not myself to have apprehended: but this one thing I do, forgetting those things which are behind, and reaching forth unto those things which are before, I press toward the mark for the prize of the high calling of God in Christ Jesus."

Isaiah 43:18-19 "Remember ye not the former things, neither consider the things of old. Behold, I will do a new thing; now it shall spring forth; shall ye not know it? I will even make a way in the wilderness, and rivers in the desert."

We are inspired by these verses to let go of the past, face the truth, and advance with faith and tenacity.

THE DENIAL DILEMMA

Psalm 139:14 1 Peter 2:9

The Denial Dilemma is a curious mystery that has perplexed philosophers and psychologists alike for millennia in the maze-like passageways of the human mind. In the face of discomfort and unwelcome realities, we as humans engage in a delicate protection mechanism that involves a complex dance of perception. Every element of our lives is impacted by this conundrum, from intimate relationships to larger societal problems. However, what precisely is the Denial Dilemma and why is it important?

Consider Mark's life as a young guy navigating the difficulties of living. Although he is endowed with limitless ability, there is a struggle with addiction that he is unable to fully address that lurks beneath the surface of his aspirations. For years, he brushes it aside, rationalizing his actions, and evading the brutal honesty that could set him free. In a world rife with societal issues, let's also contemplate a broader example—a society faced with the undeniable consequences of climate change. Denial becomes a comfortable refuge, a way to avoid the inconvenient truths that demand action and change.

In essence, the Denial Dilemma is our internal struggle with reality. When confronted with truths that go against our comfort zones, beliefs, or behaviors, humans tend to turn away from them. Furthermore, this problem is a universal one that unites all of humanity; it is not specific to any one person or society. Whether it's rejecting the suffering of a failed relationship, the effects of harmful behaviors, or the pressing nature of global concerns, denial has, at some point, provided comfort to all of us. But why should we look deeper into this difficult conundrum? The Denial Dilemma holds the key to unlocking one's capacity for personal development, assisting in developing healthier interpersonal bonds and tackling societal problems head-on and decisively. We gain the ability to transcend our bounds and face the realities that can lead us on a path to transformation by unlocking the mysteries of denial and comprehending its complex web.

So, let's start this investigation of the Denial Dilemma together, dear reader. Let's explore the complexities of the human psyche to find stories like Mark's, who was held hostage by denial until he confronted it head-on, at which point his life took a different turn. We can find the way to individual and societal enlightenment by deeply comprehending this phenomenon. This journey starts with accepting the Denial Dilemma and the profound truths it contains. The Denial Dilemma is a puzzling and frequently depressing chapter in the epic story of human life. There are times of rejection, setbacks, and disappointment in this chapter of our life stories, which many of us have experienced. These are the times when we look for chances, approval, or acknowledgment, only to receive a flat "no" or, occasionally even worse, a deafening silence. In these circumstances, it's all too simple to give in to a pervasive sense of inadequacy or unworthiness and let denial shape our perception of ourselves. But, oh, how vital it is to understand that rejection doesn't always represent a judgment of our merit.

Let's focus on the life of John, a guy with aspirations as big as the horizon's unending expanse. He desired a profession in which his talents, which had been well-tuned, would mesh with his enthusiasm. But he kept being turned down when he applied for jobs in his desired field. Unwelcome doubts crept in, whispering that he simply wasn't good enough. But John might not have completely understood that these rejections were not an accurate reflection of his worth or his skills. It's possible that the businesses he applied to were experiencing financial difficulties or that they overlooked the unique skills he had to offer. Herein lies the essence of the Denial Dilemma—the challenge of not internalizing rejection as a personal indictment. It's the capacity to discern that there are multifaceted reasons why opportunities may elude us, reasons that extend far beyond our capabilities. It's an examination of our sense of self-worth, our resilience, and our ability to maintain a positive self-perception even in the face of adversity.

The truth, my dear reader, is that when someone or something denies us, it does not diminish our inherent value. Each one of us is a masterpiece, a one-of-a-kind creation, cherished in the eyes of the Divine. Our worth transcends the spaces we fit into or the opportunities that come our way. It's an unshakable, intrinsic quality that dwells within us, unaltered by external judgments or rejections. So, let us embark on a journey to unravel the layers of the Denial Dilemma, recognizing that denial often refracts our true worth, serving as a crucible for growth, resilience, and self-discovery. In the face of rejection, may our minds be steadfast in the understanding that we are not small; we are radiant beacons of unique value in this world. The Denial Dilemma may test our resolve, but it can never dim the brilliance of our individual lights.

Psalm 139:14 "I will praise thee; for I am fearfully and wonderfully made: marvelous are thy works; and that my soul knoweth right well."

1 Peter 2:9 "But ye are a chosen generation, a royal priesthood, an holy nation, a peculiar people; that ye should shew forth the praises of him who hath called you out of darkness into his marvelous light."

God's word gives you your identity and complete worth; you cannot know yourself apart from it. These verses depict and capture our intrinsic value and individuality in God's sight, inspiring us to not let criticism or rejection from others define who we are.

RECOGNIZING THE REPEATING PATTERNS

Jeremiah 33:3 Isaiah 43:19

We frequently find ourselves navigating through a terrain characterized by recurrent patterns in the complex path of our lives. It's a phenomenon that predates all recorded history and cuts across age, culture, and experience. These patterns follow us like persistent shadows and take many different shapes, including recurring relationships, recurring failures, and even the echoes of our own decisions. The paradox comes from the fact that we are habitual, comfortable creatures by nature as humans. Because familiarity may give us a sense of security and be the root of our unhappiness.

Think about Sarah, a woman who, despite her unrelenting desire for a different ending, repeatedly finds herself in relationships that reflect the same disappointments. Or consider Robert's experiences, a man who, despite making several professional changes, is nonetheless plagued by a persistent sense of unhappiness. These stories may appear original, but there are numerous stories of other people who have been held captive by recurring patterns. Why do we keep repeating these patterns is the question that hangs over us. Why do we frequently prefer the known over the new when presented with the lessons of our past? The process of identifying recurring patterns starts here. It's an introspective journey where we peel back the layers of our lives to find the connections that tie us to these recurring themes. Because there is room for change within this investigation. We develop the ability to make deliberate decisions to break away from the cycle of recurrence, and to construct a new path that is in line with our highest hopes and wishes by becoming aware of the patterns that form our lives.

So come along with us on this journey into the essence of identifying repeated patterns, dear reader. Let's investigate the nuances of human nature, the complexity of our emotions, and the unspoken drives that lead us to familiarity. Understanding the causes of these patterns sets us on a path to self-awareness, personal development, and the potential to design a life that is not constrained by the echoes of the past but fashioned by the purpose of the present. In the artwork of our religion and daily lives, there lurks a fundamental truth that urges us to be ever aware, and ever vigilant. It's a truth that resonates strongly with believers and transcends religious and denominational lines. This truth is based on the idea that we can spot recurring patterns in our lives. As we move through life, we frequently come against recognizable difficulties, repeating roadblocks, and enduring tribulations. As Christians, we are obligated to not only identify these tendencies but also to confront and get rid of them using the might of the Bible and prayer.

Think about Anna, a devoted Christian who repeatedly encounters problems in her relationships that are mirror images of the same problems. She sees a pattern of strife and suffering that, despite her prayers for improvement, appears to continue. Or think about David's job journey, where he consistently runs into the same obstacles that prevent him from moving forward. These patterns can appear singular, but there are countless instances of Christians battling repeated issues in their life. For those who follow the path of faith, recognizing repeating patterns takes on a deeper dimension. It's a call to spiritual discernment, to be attuned to the subtle signs and signals that God may be revealing. It's an invitation to prayer, to seek divine intervention and guidance in breaking free from these cycles. When the challenges seem insurmountable, fasting becomes a powerful tool to invoke God's transformative grace.

As believers in Christ Jesus, we understand that prayer is not merely a conversation with the divine, but a conduit for change and healing. It's a means by which we can address these patterns, confront them head-on, and pray for the strength to overcome them. Fasting, too, becomes a sacred discipline, a way to deepen our connection with the divine, and to demonstrate our earnest desire for transformation. So, keep in mind that you have a powerful toolbox of prayer and faith as you begin this exploration of identifying repetitive patterns. You can discover the underlying meanings behind these patterns and, with God's mercy, break their influence on your life by being vigilant, praying earnestly, and seeking spiritual counsel. This journey involves more than just breaking free from repetitive patterns; it also involves becoming closer to God and accepting the transforming power of prayer and faith.

Jeremiah 33:3 "Call unto me, and I will answer thee, and shew thee great and mighty things, which thou knowest not."

Isaiah 43:19 "Behold, I will do a new thing; now it shall spring forth; shall ye not know it? I will even make a way in the wilderness, and rivers in the desert."

One sure thing you and I have as believers is the power of prayer and divine intervention in recognizing and breaking free from repeating patterns in their lives.

THE QUEST FOR LASTING LOVE

1 Corinthians 13:4-7 Ephesians 4:2-3

One goal stands out in the everlasting tale of human existence as both universal and intensely personal—the search for enduring love. It's a voyage that cuts through age, situation, and cultural barriers; a journey that touches the core of every person. This journey is fundamentally about our desire for a relationship that endures the test of time, a love that endures the trials of life, and a partnership that nourishes our souls.

Think about the tale of Sarah and John, two people from quite different backgrounds who were drawn together by the attraction of love. They embark on a journey, each with their own dreams and aspirations, yet united by the hope of finding something enduring. Theirs is not just a romantic tale but a reflection of the universal longing for a love that endures beyond the initial sparks and fleeting infatuations.

This quest for lasting love isn't confined to the pages of novels or the frames of Hollywood movies; it's a quest that plays out in the lives of real people. It's the single mother yearning for a partner who'll embrace her and her children with unwavering love. It's the elderly couple who've weathered decades together, their love growing deeper with each passing year. It's the young couple setting out on a new adventure, with the hope that their love will be the anchor in the uncertain seas of life. The journey towards lasting love is both exhilarating and challenging, a quest marked by moments of joy, heartache, and self-discovery. It's an exploration of vulnerability, trust, and the profound connections that make us uniquely human. In this pursuit, we uncover the eternal truth that love, though elusive at times, is a force that can transcend our limitations, heal our wounds, and bring a profound sense of fulfillment.

So, let us delve into the depths of the Quest for Lasting Love. Let us explore the intricacies of human relationships, the mysteries of the heart, and the enduring power of love itself. In this journey, we'll uncover timeless wisdom, personal stories, and insights that illuminate the path toward a love that stands the test of time—a love that, when found, becomes a treasure beyond measure. In the pursuit of human dreams and desires, there is perhaps no aspiration more universally cherished than the quest for lasting love. It's a pursuit that transcends the boundaries of culture, age, and circumstance, a journey that lies at the very core of our shared human experience. We all yearn for that profound connection, a love that defies the passage of time, and a partnership that nurtures our souls.

Think of Maria and Daniel, two souls drawn together by the intricate threads of fate. They embarked on a journey, each carrying their hopes and dreams, but united by the shared vision of lasting love. Their story isn't just one of romance; it mirrors the universal longing for a love that endures beyond fleeting infatuations and the inevitable trials of life. This pursuit of lasting love isn't confined to the pages of fairy tales or the screens of romantic movies. It's a very real quest that unfolds in the lives of ordinary people. It's the divorced father who hopes to find a companion who'll embrace his children as their own. It's the elderly couple who have weathered life's storms together, their love deepening with each passing year. It's the young couple setting out on a journey, believing that their love will be the anchor in the turbulent seas of life.

The path to lasting love is a mix of exhilarating moments and challenging trials, a journey marked by joy, heartache, and profound self-discovery. It's a quest that demands vulnerability, trust, and an unwavering commitment to nurturing the connections that make us uniquely human. And in this pursuit, we uncover a timeless truth—that love, though often elusive, is a force capable of transcending our limitations, healing our deepest wounds, and filling our lives with immeasurable richness. So come along with us as we explore The Quest for Lasting Love, dear reader. We will investigate the complex web of interpersonal relationships, the mysteries of the heart, and the enduring force of love together. On this voyage, we will discover ancient knowledge, share our tales, and gain understandings that will illuminate the way to a love that endures the test of time— a love that, once found, transforms into an inestimably valuable treasure.

1 Corinthians 13:4-7 "Charity suffereth long, and is kind; charity envieth not; charity vaunteth not itself, is not puffed up, Doth not behave itself unseemly, seeketh not her own, is not easily provoked, thinketh no evil; Rejoiceth not in iniquity, but rejoiceth in the truth; Beareth all things, believeth all things, hopeth all things, endureth all things."

Ephesians 4:2-3 "With all lowliness and meekness, with longsuffering, forbearing one another in love; Endeavouring to keep the unity of the Spirit in the bond of peace."

These verses highlight the enduring qualities of love, including patience, kindness, and the effort required to maintain unity and lasting love in relationships.

CHAPTER 2

THE COMMON THREAD

Galatians 3:28 1 Corinthians 12:26

The Common Thread, a thin but significant thread that runs through all people's experiences, can be found in the colorful tapestry of our lives. We are all connected by an underlying force that cuts over differences in culture, age, and environment. The emotions, struggles, and aspirations that bind us all together are all part of this Common Thread, which is the essence of our shared humanity. Think about Lisa, a young lady starting a new career in a busy metropolis, who must overcome formidable obstacles. She struggles with the same doubts and insecurities that have troubled so many people before her. Consider Michael, a retiree who is reflecting on a well-lived life and is troubled by the age-old issue of legacy and purpose. These narratives may seem unique, but they are but two among the countless stories of individuals navigating the ebb and flow of life's uncertainties.

The Common Thread is a unifying force that permeates every part of our existence and transcends moments of self-reflection or self-doubt. It is the delight of a child's laughing, the heartbreak of saying goodbye, the success of tenacity, and the fortitude in the face of difficulty. It is the common experience of love, grief, hope, and the intrinsic desire to find significance in life. Although it is frequently imperceptible, this thread runs through all human experience. It acts as a continual reminder that despite our differences, we have a strong bond in common—a shared humanity that unites us. Recognizing the Common Thread allows us to celebrate the magnificence of our common experience, the power of our community, and the enduring resiliency of the human heart.

Let's explore the nuances of our mutual experiences, shared joys, and shared difficulties as we start this mutual Thread exploration. We get insights into the richness of life itself by honoring the essence of our humanity because we find comfort and inspiration in this shared fabric. Let's explore the experiences, feelings, and goals that connect us all in the vivid mosaic of our existence.

There is a subtle, almost ethereal presence in the enormous, interwoven tapestry of human existence—a thread that unites us all, despite our varied origins and unique travels. Our shared experiences, feelings, and goals are woven into the fabric of what is referred to as the Common Thread. It is the intangible connection that underscores our shared humanity, a universal force that transcends the boundaries of time, place, and culture.

Imagine the story of Tom, a hardworking farmer in a remote village, toiling under the same sun that warms the shoulders of bustling city dwellers like Emily, a young executive chasing her dreams in a high-rise office. Despite the stark differences in their lives, they both share a deep-rooted connection to the land, an understanding of the rhythm of seasons, and a profound longing for a well-lived life. This is the essence of the Common Thread—a bridge that links seemingly disparate lives through shared experiences and common emotions. The Common Thread, however, is not limited to the overarching stories of existence. It appears in the simplest moments and the commonplace events that affect us all. It is the comfort of a stranger's smile on a trying day, the shared joy of laughter, and the stillness of empathy during challenging times that binds us together. The human spirit is characterized by the pursuit of love, the search for meaning, fortitude in the face of difficulty, and unwavering optimism.

This thread is woven into the very fabric of our lives, although it is frequently invisible. It serves as a subtle reminder that, behind it all, we are all connected by a journey—a journey characterized by a commonality of experiences that define our humanity. In recognizing the Common Thread, we discover a profound sense of belonging, a source of strength in our shared struggles, and a wellspring of inspiration in our collective triumphs. So, dear reader, as we embark on this exploration of the Common Thread, let us delve deeper into the intricacies of our shared existence, the universal joys, and the challenges that unite us all. Together, let us unravel the stories, emotions, and aspirations that connect us in the grand mosaic of our lives.

Galatians 3:28 "There is neither Jew nor Greek, there is neither bond nor free, there is neither male nor female: for ye are all one in Christ Jesus."

1 Corinthians 12:26 "And whether one member suffer, all the members suffer with it; or one member be honoured, all the members rejoice with it."

These verses emphasize the idea of unity and interconnectedness among people, highlighting the commonality that transcends differences.

LOVE KNOWS NO BOUNDARIES

John 15:13 1 Corinthians 13:4-7

Love is a force that knows no bounds and an essence that transcends geography, culture, and situation in the complex dance of human emotions. Love is a global language that speaks to the very essence of our humanity and has the limitless power to unite people, cross barriers, and link hearts. It is a force that crosses national boundaries, defying geographical restrictions and eradicating prejudice-based obstacles. The common thread that reminds us that we are all fundamentally social beings who desire acceptance and connection is love, in all its varied manifestations. Picture the story of Maria and Ahmed, two souls hailing from distant lands, separated by oceans and cultures. Despite the oceans that physically separate them, they found in each other a kindred spirit, a connection that transcended borders. Their love story, like countless others, illustrates the profound truth that love knows no geographical confines. It's the embrace of a parent cradling their child, the bond of friendship forged across continents, and the romantic union of hearts that beat as one.

Love Knows No Boundaries is not just about romantic love; it's a celebration of love in all its forms. It's the unwavering support of friends during life's storms, the compassion of strangers lending a helping hand, and the enduring bonds of family that defy the tests of time. Love, with its transformative power, shows us that we are, at our core, connected by the universal language of the heart. In exploring the theme of Love Knows No Boundaries, let us go through the intricate web of human relationships, a journey that reveals the remarkable ability of love to overcome the divisions that often separate us. It examines the limitless power of love—the love that unites people, inspires them, and serves as a constant reminder of our shared humanity. Let me alleviate your mind and help you. We will discover the joyful and inspiring instances of love's capacity to transcend boundaries and unite people as we delve into the tales, experiences, and feelings that make up Love Knows No Boundaries. By doing this, we acknowledge the bond that unites us all and demonstrate that, in the vast fabric of our life as humans, love has no bounds. A powerful, all-pervasive force known as love exists in the complex web of human relationships, defying the very idea of bounds. In its most pure state, love is a limitless force that is not constrained by the boundaries of place, culture, or situation. A force that transcends the obstacles that might normally keep us apart, it is a universal language that speaks to the depths of our shared humanity. At its core, love is an unrelenting dedication to the pleasure and well-being of others—a selfless gift of ourselves made in an effort to bring out the best in people we cherish.

Think about the tale of Sarah and David, two souls whose paths crossed in the most unlikely of ways. David, a modest farmer from a small village, and Sarah, who was from a busy city, met. They found in one another a profound connection, a love that could not be contained by the confines of their worlds, despite the gap of differences that might have separated them. Their relationship is an example of the selfless nature of love, where one is prepared to sacrifice oneself for the benefit of the other.

But Love Knows No Boundaries goes far beyond only romantic relationships. It is the unwavering support of a friend who stands by your side through thick and thin, the compassion of a stranger who extends a helping hand in a time of need, and the unbreakable bonds of family that endure through life's trials. It is the purest form of selflessness, an act of giving that seeks the ultimate good in others. In delving into the theme of Love Knows No Boundaries, we embark on a journey through the intricate labyrinth of human relationships. It is a journey that reveals the remarkable capacity of love to overcome the divisions and limitations that often threaten to separate us. It is an exploration of love's boundless nature—a force that unites, uplifts, and reminds us of our shared humanity.

So, let's start the investigation together, my reader. We shall discover the joyful and amazing instances of love's capacity to overcome all obstacles and unite people as we journey through the experiences, stories, and emotions that make up Love Knows No Boundaries. By doing this, we celebrate the unifying power that unites us all and demonstrates that, in the glorious fabric of our human experience, love has no bounds.

John 15:13 "Greater love has no one than this: to lay down one's life for one's friends."

1 Corinthians 13:4-7 "Love is patient, love is kind. It does not envy, it does not boast, it is not proud. It does not dishonor others, it is not self-seeking, it is not easily angered, it keeps no record of wrongs. Love does not delight in evil but rejoices with the truth. It always protects, always trusts, always hopes, always perseveres."

The sacrificial nature of love is our character, where giving of oneself for the well-being of others is seen as the highest expression of love.

ATTRACTING THE SAME TYPES

There is frequently a puzzling phenomenon—a propensity to draw the same kinds of people into our lives—in the complicated tapestry of our personal relationships. It's a recurring motif that appears in numerous stories, a pattern that cuts over age, culture, and location barriers. We often find ourselves drawn to people who reflect familiar traits, both positive and negative, which is both fascinating and frustrating. In the world of interpersonal relationships, we are like magnets, drawing others to us who share traits, preferences, and life experiences with us.

Consider the story of Anna, a kind-hearted soul who repeatedly finds herself in relationships with partners who share similar characteristics. Despite her best intentions, she seems to gravitate toward individuals who, in some way, echo the same patterns. Or think of Robert, a driven professional who, despite changing jobs and industries, encounters similar dynamics in his workplace relationships. Their narratives may differ, but their experiences of attracting the same types are remarkably similar. This phenomenon isn't limited to romantic entanglements alone; it permeates various facets of our lives. We may notice it in the recurring themes of friendships, professional interactions, or even the dynamics within our families. It's as if there's an unseen force at play, guiding us toward those who reflect our own inner complexities and unresolved issues.

Attracting the same types is a puzzle that begs exploration—an inquiry into the depths of human psychology and the complexities of our desires and insecurities. It's a journey that delves into the subconscious realms of our hearts, seeking to unearth the hidden motivations that draw us to individuals who mirror our own qualities, both light and shadow. Together, we will sort through the complexities of this phenomenon by looking at the patterns that appear in our interpersonal interactions and attempting to decipher the more profound signals they contain. By doing this, we may discover important truths that not only illuminate how we relate to one another but also offer a chance for personal development, self-awareness, and ultimately, the potential for stronger, more satisfying relationships.

A strange thread that draws us repeatedly to draw the same kinds of individuals into our orbit often runs through the intricate patterns of our connections in the vast tapestry that is our lives. It's a curious and, at times, confounding phenomenon that traverses the landscape of human connection, transcending age, culture, and circumstance. This peculiar pattern is akin to encountering familiar faces in a crowded room, as if the universe conspires to bring us together with those who mirror qualities, both constructive and perplexing, that strike an uncanny chord within us. Enter the life of Emily, a spirited adventurer whose pursuit of love continually leads her into relationships with individuals who share strikingly similar traits. Despite her best intentions and hopes for diversity, she finds herself in the embrace of those who echo the same dynamics she thought she'd left behind. Or consider the journey of James, a dedicated professional who, despite relocating and changing jobs, grapples with analogous interpersonal challenges in each new chapter of his career. Their stories may diverge in detail, but the theme of attracting the same types resonates universally.

Beyond romantic relationships, this phenomenon also affects friendships, professional networks, and even family dynamics. We are drawn to people who embody the complexity, desires, and unfinished narratives of our own inner selves by an unseen attraction. Our conscious intents and the hidden currents of our subconscious engage in an odd dance. We are prompted to reflect on the complexities of human psychology and the hidden layers of our needs, fears, and secret longings when we attract people who are similar to us. It is an effort to solve the riddle of why we are pulled repeatedly to people who possess the same recognizable traits, both enlightening and murky. Together, we will unravel the intricate threads that weave through our personal relationships, seeking not just to understand the patterns that emerge but also to glean valuable insights. These insights may hold the key to our own growth, self-awareness, and the possibility of forging more enlightened, nurturing, and harmonious connections with those who cross our path in the grand mosaic of life.

Proverbs 26:11 "As a dog returneth to his vomit, so a fool returneth to his folly."

2 Corinthians 6:14 "Be ye not unequally yoked together with unbelievers: for what fellowship hath righteousness with unrighteousness? and what communion hath light with darkness?"

These verses offer insights into patterns of behavior and the importance of being mindful of the types of connections we form in our lives.

BREAKING DOWN STEREOTYPES

James 2:1-4 Galatians 3:28

Stereotypes frequently throw a shadow in the intricate web of human interaction—a shadow that obscures our perceptions, tints our assessments, and shapes our interactions. We frequently lump people into neat, established categories based on their appearance, background, or affiliations because of these preconceived conceptions, which are the result of a variety of influences.

The diversity of our experiences, the depth of our individual tales, and the complexity of our identities, however, are what truly define our shared humanity.

Meet Sarah, a brave young woman who challenges the preconceived notions people have about her line of work. Due to her gender, she often encounters doubts about her computer engineering skills. However, she has created her own route and broken free from these restrictions to become a success in her area. Or think about Ahmed, whose cultural background has occasionally caused others to draw broad conclusions about his beliefs and values. He is a canvas painted with the vivid hues of his uniqueness despite these presumptions. A voyage into the core of our common human experience, Breaking Down Stereotypes aims to separate the strands of prejudice and misunderstanding. It's an exploration of the stories, both personal and collective, that have shaped our perceptions and fueled our biases. It's a testament to the individuals who defy stereotypes every day, who rise above preconceived notions to showcase the true depth and diversity of human potential.

But this journey is not just about understanding the dynamics of stereotypes; it's a call to action. It's an invitation to challenge the status quo, to question our own assumptions, and to embrace the beauty of our individual and collective identities. It's about opening our hearts and minds to the mosaic of human experiences, recognizing that each person is a unique blend of stories, talents, and dreams. I want to bring you to understand the origins of our biases, to celebrate the individuals who defy stereotypes, and to foster a world where the richness of human diversity is not hindered by rigid categories. In doing so, we hope to create a future where stereotypes are but distant echoes in the vast symphony of our shared humanity, and where the uniqueness of each individual shines brilliantly in its own right. Stereotypes frequently operate as obstacles in the complex web of human connection, blocking the free flow of understanding and casting doubt on our perceptions and judgments. These preconceived ideas, fostered by a wide range of factors, tend to categorize people according to their appearances, backgrounds, or affiliations. The colorful tapestry of varied experiences, rich personal histories, and the complexity of our identities lie at the core of our shared existence.

Meet Alex, a young artist who might not be following the standards of society. When Alex discusses pursuing a career in the arts, there is sometimes a raised eyebrow or a puzzled expression, as if that doesn't fit the template. Yet, within the strokes of a paintbrush or the notes of a melody, Alex defies these stereotypes, proving that creativity knows no predefined boundaries. Or consider the story of Maria, who carries with her a name associated with a particular culture. However, her identity is a mosaic, reflecting influences from various corners of the world. In her, one finds a unique blend of cultures, challenging the idea that a name can encapsulate a person's entirety. Breaking Down Stereotypes is a voyage into the heart of our shared human tapestry—a journey that beckons us to unravel the threads of prejudice and misunderstanding. It's an expedition through the stories, both intimate and societal, that have woven the fabric of our perceptions and perpetuated our biases. It's a tribute to those who defy stereotypes daily, who shatter the preconceived notions to reveal the true richness and diversity of human potential.

Yet, this journey is not confined to observation alone; it's an impassioned call to action. It's an entreaty to challenge the status quo, to scrutinize our own preconceptions, and to embrace the intricate beauty of our individual and collective identities. It invites us to open our hearts and minds to the kaleidoscope of human experiences, acknowledging that each person is a living testament to a unique blend of stories, talents, and aspirations. Breaking Down Stereotypes, let us embark together. Let us strive to discern the roots of our biases, to honor the resilience of those who defy stereotypes, and to foster a world where the magnificence of human diversity flourishes unhindered by rigid categories. Through this journey, we aspire to forge a future where stereotypes are but echoes of the past, where everyone's uniqueness radiates brilliantly, illuminating the grand tapestry of our shared humanity.

James 2:1-4 "My brethren, have not the faith of our Lord Jesus Christ, the Lord of glory, with respect of persons. For if there come unto your assembly a man with a gold ring, in goodly apparel, and there come in also a poor man in vile raiment; And ye have respect to him that weareth the gay clothing, and say unto him, Sit thou here in a good place; and say to the poor, Stand thou there, or sit here under my footstool: Are ye not then partial in yourselves, and are become judges of evil thoughts?"

Galatians 3:28 "There is neither Jew nor Greek, there is neither bond nor free, there is neither male nor female: for ye are all one in Christ Jesus."

These verses underscore the importance of not showing favoritism or making distinctions based on external appearances or societal categories, highlighting the need for fair and equal treatment of all individuals.

CHAPTER 3

THE FEAR OF LONELINESS

Isaiah 41:10 Psalm 34:17

There is a powerful and common sensation known as the Fear of Loneliness that occurs in the quiet periods of our lives when the bustling commotion of the outside world fades. It's a feeling that knows no bounds, an underlying human terror that dwells in the depths of our hearts and is frequently covered up by layers of daily life. This anxiety expresses our deep need for company, connection, and the consoling presence of others during this life journey.

Imagine the life of Mark, a man who has been successful professionally and is surrounded by friends, but who frequently struggles with a deep loneliness as the day ends. Or consider Sarah, a senior citizen who has experienced both joy and grief over the course of her long life, yet despite these emotions, loneliness still haunts her, casting a shadow over her later years. The fear of loneliness connects them, as it does many others around the world, despite the differences in their personal histories.

The fear of loneliness goes deeper than just the anxiety associated with being physically alone. The fear of being alone, rejected, or ignored—even in the middle of a busy room—is what it is. It's the nagging concern that our existence might lack meaning without the presence of others to share it with. It's the quiet vulnerability that surfaces when we confront the prospect of growing old or facing life's trials without a support system. This fear, though often unspoken, carries profound weight in our lives. It serves as a reminder that we are social beings, wired to seek connections with others. It prompts us to reach out, to build bridges, and to nurture relationships that sustain us in times of need. Yet, it can also manifest as a shadow, driving us to make choices or compromises that aren't in our best interest, simply to avoid the perceived solitude.

Together, we will navigate the depths of human connection, uncover the sources of this fear, and find insights that empower us to embrace solitude when it comes, while still nurturing the relationships that bring warmth and meaning to our lives. The specific concept of "The Fear of Loneliness" is not directly addressed in the Bible. However, you can find scriptures that touch on related themes of fear, comfort, and God's presence. Here are;

Isaiah 41:10 "Fear thou not; for I am with thee: be not dismayed; for I am thy God: I will strengthen thee; yea, I will help thee; yea, I will uphold thee with the right hand of my righteousness."

Psalm 34:17 "The righteous cry, and the LORD heareth, and delivereth them out of all their troubles."

While these verses may not explicitly mention "The Fear of Loneliness," they emphasize the comforting presence of God and the assurance that God is with us in times of fear and loneliness.

THE LONELINESS PARADOX

Psalm 25:16 Psalm 68:6

A paradoxical thread that runs through the fabric of our lives and is both soothing and unsettling in its presence can be found in the tapestry of human emotions. The Loneliness conundrum is the name of this conundrum. It's a complicated interaction between loneliness and connection, a feeling that is both broadly shared and intensely personal. In its core, The Loneliness Paradox tells the tale of our never-ending search for connection in a society that simultaneously appears more connected than ever while also feeling lonelier.

Think about Sarah, a young professional who is happy and successful in a busy metropolis. She travels through a paradoxical journey while being surrounded by a flurry of social interactions, never-ending notifications, and virtual acquaintances. She yearns for simplicity in the midst of the nonstop digital buzz. Or ponder the story of George, an elderly man whose world has become increasingly quiet with the passage of time. In the solitude of his days, he reflects on the depth of human connection he once knew, yearning for a simple, genuine connection that seems increasingly elusive. The Loneliness Paradox is not a contradiction of terms but a reflection of the intricate human experience. It's the experience of being in a crowded room yet feeling profoundly alone or finding solace in solitary moments while yearning for meaningful companionship. It's the contradiction of living in a digitally connected age where people are always just a message away, yet the feeling of loneliness persists like a distant ache.

This paradox touches on the core of our humanity—the innate need for genuine connections, for meaningful conversations, and for relationships that nurture our souls. It reminds us that, amid the hustle and bustle of our lives, we must also cherish the moments of solitude, self-reflection, and inner peace. It challenges us to strike a delicate balance between the exhilarating noise of the external world and the quiet wisdom that can be found within ourselves. So, brace up as you and I explore The Loneliness Paradox together, let us navigate the intricacies of this deeply human experience. Let us delve into the stories, emotions, and insights that define it, embracing both the power of connection and the richness of solitude. In doing so, we may uncover the keys to finding harmony within this paradox, forging genuine connections in a connected world, and discovering the beauty in both the presence and absence of others in our lives.

The concept of "The Loneliness Paradox" is not explicitly addressed in the Bible, so there are no specific scriptures that explicitly mention it. However, you can find relevant verses that touch on related themes of loneliness, companionship, and God's presence. However, these two will suffice. Psalm 25:16 "Turn thee unto me, and have mercy upon me; for I am desolate and afflicted."

Psalm 68:6 "God setteth the solitary in families: he bringeth out those which are bound with chains: but the rebellious dwell in a dry land."

While these verses may not directly address "The Loneliness Paradox," they do touch on the feelings of loneliness and the comfort and companionship that can be found in God.

OVERCOMING THE FEAR

2 Timothy 1:7 Isaiah 41:10

The Fear of the Unknown is a recurring tune in the grand symphony of human existence that resonates with many people. It's a fear that keeps us bound to the safe, secure, and familiar while enveloping unknown terrain in darkness. The indomitable spirit that refuses to be constrained by fear and yearns for growth, discovery, and the thrill of venturing beyond the bounds of the familiar yet arises as we stand on the edge of the unknown. Think about Emily, a young woman who must make a significant choice for her future. Long shadows were cast over her path by the dread of potential failure, the uncertainty of change, and the fear of the unknown. Nevertheless, she understands that remaining put out of fear will never help her achieve her goals. Or think about Thomas' journey as he considers making a significant life change and taking a plunge into the unknown. It is obvious that he is terrified of leaving behind the protection of his routine and exploring uncharted territory. He is aware, however, that the other side of fear is frequently where real growth can be found.

A trip that encourages us to face our fear head-on, accept it as it is, and then move forward bravely is Overcoming the Fear. It explores this common human emotion. It is the understanding that fear, while natural, need not act as a constant anchor. Realizing that fear can be a force that propels us into the undiscovered waters of possibilities. Fear may be a catalyst for transformation. The goal of this voyage is to embrace fear as a traveling partner on the road to personal development. It is accepting the anxious moments of uncertainty and utilizing them as fire to get toward our goals. It's about summoning the inner strength to challenge the status quo, to break free from the chains of comfort, and to pursue our dreams with unwavering determination. Let's explore the core of human courage together as we work toward the mastery of overpowering fear. Let's honor the experiences of people who overcame fear head-on and came out stronger. Let's explore the ideas and techniques that help us face our anxieties, navigate the new area of our goals, and find the perseverance to press on even when the road ahead is uncertain. By doing this, we might find that, despite our fears, we are capable of amazing feats and opening the doors to a future brimming with opportunities.

2 Timothy 1:7 "For God hath not given us the spirit of fear; but of power, and of love, and of a sound mind."

Isaiah 41:10 "Fear thou not; for I am with thee: be not dismayed; for I am thy God: I will strengthen thee; yea, I will help thee; yea, I will uphold thee with the right hand of my righteousness."

These scriptures offer encouragement and reassurance that, through faith and trust, we can overcome fear and find strength and courage.

EMBRACING SOLITUDE

Psalm 46:10 Matthew 6:6

Amidst the clamor and bustle of our modern lives, there lies an oft-neglected and profound truth —the art of Embracing Solitude. In a world that values constant connection, busy schedules, and a relentless pursuit of external stimuli, solitude is often feared, misunderstood, or altogether avoided. However, within the quiet embrace of solitude, there is an opportunity to uncover the depths of our inner selves, to find solace, and to nurture a profound sense of peace and self-awareness. Imagine the story of Anna, a vibrant young woman who constantly juggles her career, social commitments, and digital engagements. Yet, in the quiet moments of solitude, she discovers a sanctuary—a place where she can reflect, recharge, and truly listen to her inner voice. Or consider the life of David, an adventurer at heart who craves the thrill of exploration. But it is in the stillness of solitude, when he's alone with his thoughts, that he discovers the greatest adventures can occur within the corridors of his own mind.

Embracing Solitude is a journey into the heart of our inner world—a journey that beckons us to turn our gaze inward, to explore the landscapes of our thoughts, emotions, and dreams. It's an invitation to seek the comfort and wisdom that can only be found in the company of our own selves. It is an acknowledgment that, amidst the cacophony of external demands and distractions, solitude is not a foe to be feared but a friend to be cherished. Solitude is not about isolation; it's about finding harmony within our own company. It's about recognizing that, in the absence of external distractions, we have the space to rediscover our passions, hear our inner wisdom, and cultivate a sense of inner peace that can sustain us in the face of life's challenges. It's about fostering self-compassion, self-reflection, and self-love—a practice that can lead to a deeper connection with others and a more meaningful engagement with the world.

Let's embark on a journey of self-discovery together as we examine Embracing Solitude. Let's honor the experiences of individuals who have found comfort in isolation and discover the innate wisdom that endures throughout time. And let us be aware that when we embrace solitude, we are not withdrawing from the world but rather becoming closer to our true selves, ensuring that our actions are in line with our beliefs, and cultivating an inner sense of contentment that has the potential to profoundly improve our lives.

Psalm 46:10 "Be still, and know that I am God: I will be exalted among the heathen, I will be exalted in the earth."

Matthew 6:6 "But thou, when thou prayest, enter into thy closet, and when thou hast shut thy door, pray to thy Father which is in secret; and thy Father which seeth in secret shall reward thee openly."

These verses emphasize the value of stillness, introspection, and finding a quiet space for reflection and connection, both with oneself and with a higher spiritual presence.

CHAPTER 4

UNMASKING YOUR DESIRES

Psalm 37:4 Jeremiah 29:11

A fascinating mystery—the world of Unmasking Your Desires—exists within the complex dance of human existence. It's a quest to uncover the layers of society's expectations, a voyage into the depths of our deepest desires, and a revelation of our genuine dreams. These passions hold the secrets to our greatest fulfillment and authenticity, sometimes concealed beneath the masks we wear in daily life.

Think about Michael, a loving father and hardworking corporate employee who has long delayed pursuing his aspirations. He masks a burning desire to pursue his passion for painting under the guise of duty and responsibility. Or reflect on the life of Lisa, a successful entrepreneur known for her unwavering determination. Beyond the façade of success, she harbors a secret yearning for a simpler, more balanced life, away from the relentless pursuit of achievement. Unmasking Your Desires is a journey of self-discovery that invites us to identify our passions, free from external expectations and social pressures. It's an investigation of the inner needs that are frequently masked by the bustle of daily life. These aspirations are the core of our authenticity and the compass that directs us toward meaningful lives.

It's not about ignoring obligations or impracticality on this journey. It involves realizing that when our desires are revealed and understood, they can guide our decisions in a way that is consistent with our deepest values. It's about having the courage to dream, to go for what inspires us, and to realize all our potential. So, as we explore Unmasking Your Desires, let's take a voyage into the world of self-discovery together, dear reader. Let's honor those who have overcome societal expectations to accept their real goals by honoring their inspiring stories. And let's acknowledge that by being honest about our ambitions, we not only achieve fulfillment but also give the world a gift of our most genuine selves, serving as a beacon of hope for others to pursue their dreams.

The concept of "Unmasking Your Desires" is not explicitly addressed in the Bible, so there are no specific scriptures that explicitly mention it. However, you can find verses that touch on related themes of seeking one's heart's desires, authenticity, and finding purpose.

Psalm 37:4 "Delight thyself also in the Lord, and he shall give thee the desires of thine heart."

Jeremiah 29:11 "For I know the thoughts that I think toward you, saith the Lord, thoughts of peace, and not of evil, to give you an expected end."

While these verses may not directly address the concept of unmasking desires, they emphasize the importance of seeking one's heart's desires in alignment with a deeper spiritual connection and divine purpose.

DEFINIG YOUR IDEAL PARTNER

There is a timeless quest that frequently occupies the minds and hearts of many people in the complex fabric of their lives: the effort to define their ideal partner. It is an exploration of the traits and qualities that speak to our souls and one that cuts over cultural, age, and background boundaries. In addition to romantic longing, finding this perfect spouse involves delving deeply into our underlying beliefs, aspirations, and the deep need for a compatible travel buddy in life.

Imagine the life of Sarah, a creative young woman who longs to travel and create art. When she thinks about her ideal companion, she imagines a like-minded somebody who will inspire her with their passion for creativity and adventure. Or think about John, a committed professional who is looking for a partner to help him create a meaningful life in line with his ideals and aspirations for the future, not just for companionship.

Defining Your Ideal Partner is a voyage into the heart of self-discovery—a journey that prompts us to reflect on our character, desires, and what truly matters to us. It's an exploration of the qualities that complement our personalities, support our growth, and make us feel cherished and understood. It's an acknowledgment that finding an ideal partner extends beyond superficial attributes; it's about shared values, common goals, and emotional resonance. This journey isn't solely about creating a checklist of desired traits; it's about understanding ourselves and what we bring to a relationship. It's about recognizing that, while an ideal partner might not be perfect, they should be perfectly suited to our unique blend of quirks, strengths, and vulnerabilities. It's about seeking a connection that transcends physical attraction and delves into the depths of emotional compatibility.

So, my beloved, let us celebrate the stories of those who have found love that aligns with their true selves and aspirations. Let us recognize that, in defining our ideal partner, we not only seek a life companion but also a reflection of our own evolving journey—a partner who supports our growth, shares our dreams, and adds to the richness of our life's narrative.

DIFFERENTIATING BETWEEN WANTS AND NEEDS

Philippians 4:11-12 Matthew 6:31-33

Differentiating between wants and needs is a critical ability that often dictates the direction of our lives amid the complex mosaic of our wishes. It's a trip into the core of our dreams, an effort to sort through the clamor of wishes in our heads to determine what counts. This ability is about finding clarity, balance, and contentment in our quest for a happy life, not only differentiating between unimportant wants and necessary needs.

Take Mark's story, a young professional navigating his career in a busy city. As he navigates through a world of endless choices and opportunities, he grapples with the distinction between what he wants—a lavish lifestyle—and what he truly needs—meaningful connections and a sense of purpose. Or think of Sarah, a single parent working tirelessly to provide for her family. In her life, the line between wants and needs is often blurred, yet she knows that nurturing her children's well-being is paramount, while other desires may have to wait. A voyage into the depths of our values, Differentiating Between Wants and Needs invites us to consider what is consistent with our fundamental principles and long-term objectives. It is a study of the elements that support our health, foster our development, and improve our interpersonal connections. It acknowledges that, despite their validity, our wants sometimes cause us to deviate and focus less on the essential requirements that feed our souls.

This path isn't about depriving ourselves of life's pleasures; rather, it's about making deliberate decisions that prioritize what counts. It's about recognizing that our needs form the foundation of our contentment and happiness, while our wants add flavor and variety to our existence. It's about finding a harmonious balance between the two, a balance that allows us to savor life's blessings without losing sight of what's essential. Differentiating Between Wants and Needs, let us journey together into the realm of self-awareness and mindful decision-making. Let us celebrate the stories of those who have found fulfillment by aligning their choices with their deepest needs. And let us recognize that, in mastering this skill, we not only navigate life's complexities with greater wisdom but also cultivate a profound sense of contentment and gratitude for the abundance that surrounds us.

Philippians 4:11-12 "Not that I speak in respect of want: for I have learned, in whatsoever state I am, therewith to be content. I know both how to be abased, and I know how to abound:
everywhere and in all things I am instructed both to be full and to be hungry, both to abound and to suffer need."

Matthew 6:31-33 "Therefore take no thought, saying, What shall we eat? or, What shall we drink? or, Wherewithal shall we be clothed? (For after all these things do the Gentiles seek:) for your heavenly Father knoweth that ye have need of all these things. But seek ye first the kingdom of God, and his righteousness; and all these things shall be added unto you."

These verses stress the value of finding fulfillment in higher spiritual qualities as opposed to just material desires, pursuing the kingdom of God, and being content. They emphasize the idea that we can achieve contentment and obtain the blessings we need by setting priorities that are in line with our real needs and spiritual development.

SEEKING GOD'S WILL IN YOUR DESIRES

The process of seeking God's will in your desires happens inside the broad landscape of our desires. A spiritual journey into the core of our desires goes beyond the bounds of personal aspirations. This path isn't just about going after what we want; it's also about figuring out what fits with God's divine design for our life and striking a balance between our wants and the bigger goal that calls to us from a higher power. Imagine the story of Emily, a compassionate soul with a deep yearning to make a difference in the world. As she navigates her career choices and life's path, she's mindful of seeking God's guidance in her desires, knowing that her inner callings are not just random whims but potential instruments of God's grace. Or think of Thomas, a man of faith who looks to divine wisdom as he contemplates major life decisions. He understands that seeking God's will in his desires requires surrendering to a higher purpose and being open to the unexpected ways in which it might manifest.

Seeking God's Will in Your Desires is an odyssey into the realm of divine guidance—a journey that beckons us to pause and listen to the still, small voice within. It's an exploration of the desires that stir our hearts, recognizing that they may be signposts pointing toward God's intentions for our lives. It's an acknowledgment that, as we cultivate a relationship with the Divine, our desires can become vessels of love, compassion, and positive change in the world. The goal of this trip is to invite God into the very center of our dreams rather than to give up on them. It involves evaluating if our wants are consistent with love, generosity, and fairness and whether they advance human progress and our spiritual development. It involves asking for insight via prayer, thought, and meditation, allowing spiritual direction to illuminate our way, and taking solace in the awareness that God may use our innermost desires to further his purposes. Let us celebrate the stories of those who have found divine purpose in their desires and discovered the joy of serving a higher calling. Let us recognize that, in seeking God's will, we not only fulfill our potential but also become agents of divine grace, manifesting love, compassion, and transformation in the world around us.

Proverbs 3:5-6 "Trust in the Lord with all thine heart; and lean not unto thine own understanding.
In all thy ways acknowledge him, and he shall direct thy paths."

Psalm 37:4 "Delight thyself also in the Lord, and he shall give thee the desires of thine heart."

These verses emphasize the importance of trusting in God's guidance and seeking His wisdom in all aspects of life, including our desires. They suggest that when we align our desires with God's will and trust in His direction, we can find fulfillment and see our heart's desires fulfilled in accordance with His divine plan.

CHAPTER 5

SELF-LOVE AND SELF-WORTH

There is a crucial chapter in the complex road of self-discovery and personal development, the chapter of self-love and self-worth. It is a story that every person, regardless of age or origin, encounters, and shapes throughout their lifetime. This chapter explores the core of who we are and how we view ourselves in a world that frequently inundates us with expectations and judgments, going far beyond brief moments of self-appreciation or the flimsy façade of self-esteem.

Think about Sarah, a young lady who for years let other people's perceptions of her determine her sense of value. She sought validation from external sources, often neglecting her inner voice and feelings. Yet, as time passed, she embarked on a transformative journey of self-love—a journey that invited her to recognize her inherent worth and love herself, flaws, and all. Or think of John, a man who had faced setbacks and failures, leading to moments of self-doubt and insecurity. But through the power of self-love, he discovered that his worth wasn't tied to his achievements, but to the unique person he was becoming. Self-Love and Self-Worth are more than just ideas; they are the cornerstones of our well-being and pleasure. This trip is an investigation into the love we show to ourselves, recognizing that we are worthy of acceptance, kindness, and compassion. It's a recognition that our value is inherent to who we are and not dependent on approval from others.

This journey is about accepting our flaws rather than striving for perfection. It's not about being conceited or arrogant; it's about taking care of and being compassionate toward oneself. The relationship we have with ourselves sets the tone for all our other relationships, therefore it's important to nurture that relationship and quiet the inner critic, replace self-doubt with self-assurance, and do so. So, my beloved partner, let us take a journey together into the world of self-compassion and acceptance as we begin this examination of self-love and self-worth. Let's honor the experiences of those who have found resilience and strength in loving themselves. And let's acknowledge that as we learn to cherish and respect ourselves, we not only take care of our well-being but also transform into shining examples of compassion, benevolence, and empowerment for others around us.

UNDERSTANDING SELF-LOVE

There is a fundamental essence—a force that has the power to reshape lives and relationships— within the complex tapestry of the human experience. Understanding Self-Love is the name of this essence, which is a path of self-reflection, acceptance, and compassion for the one person we frequently ignore: ourselves. Think about Lisa, a cheerful young lady who gave selflessly to others but rarely showed any kindness to herself. Her life was a never-ending frenzy of fulfilling obligation upon obligation, leaving her exhausted and unsatisfied. As she started down the road of Understanding Self-Love, she realized that real love and compassion must start from the inside out.

Understanding self-love goes beyond indulgent narcissism or self-centeredness. That we must first love and care for ourselves to properly love and care for others is a profound insight. It's about appreciating our inherent worth and realizing that self-love is the cornerstone of all other kinds of love. This path isn't about haughtiness or entitlement; rather, it's about accepting who we are and taking care of our wellbeing. It involves quieting the inner critic who finds fault with everything we do and substituting a voice of self-compassion for it. Understanding that we are unique and worthwhile persons rather than being defined by our flaws, appearance, or accomplishments. Understanding Self-Love invites us to embrace our imperfections, for they make us beautifully human. It teaches us to set healthy boundaries that protect our emotional and mental health, allowing us to engage in relationships from a place of strength rather than neediness. It encourages us to prioritize self-care and self-compassion, recognizing that these acts of love are not selfish but essential for our overall well-being.

So, dear reader, let's journey together into the world of self-compassion and self-acceptance as we begin this examination of Understanding Self-Love. Let's celebrate the success stories of those who have discovered freedom and happiness by learning to love themselves. And let us remember that by developing self-love, we not only improve our own lives but also serve as examples of love and inspiration to a world that desperately needs more tolerance and acceptance.

DISCOVERING YOUR WORTH IN CHRIST

There is a turning point for many people in the great fabric of human existence—a moment of tremendous awakening and transformation. It's a path called "Discovering Your Worth in Christ" that goes beyond self-doubt, insecurity, and outside approval. The goal of this journey is to help you grasp your worth as a prized creation in the eyes of a loving and divine Creator, not only how valuable you are as a human. Imagine the story of James, a man who spent years seeking validation in his career, relationships, and material possessions. He often felt inadequate and restless, yearning for a sense of significance that constantly eluded him. However, as he embarked on the path of discovering his worth in Christ, he realized that his worth was not contingent on external achievements or others' opinions but was an inherent part of his identity as a beloved child of God.

Finding Your Value in Christ is a journey of the soul into the depths of your nature. Beyond your duties and identities, you come to understand how much a Higher Power values and loves you. It is the knowledge that God's constant love and grace, not your accomplishments or shortcomings, determine your value. You are invited to let go of the weights of perfectionism and self-criticism because of this journey by realizing that you are sufficient just the way you are. As you realize that you have already received validation from your Creator, it encourages you to let go of the desire for ongoing approval from other people. It teaches you to freely give yourself the same love, compassion, and forgiveness as God does.

Discovering Your Worth in Christ is not about ego or pride; it's about embracing humility and gratitude for the immeasurable love bestowed upon you. It's a realization that your worth is not a result of your efforts but a divine gift that you carry within you. It's an invitation to live a life rooted in purpose and meaning, knowing that your worth is not determined by circumstances but by your identity as a beloved creation of God. In this exploration of Discovering Your Worth in Christ, let us journey together into the realm of spiritual awakening and self-acceptance. Let us celebrate the stories of those who have found peace, purpose, and unwavering worth in their faith. And let us recognize that, in discovering your worth in Christ, you not only find solace and purpose but also become a beacon of light, reflecting God's love and grace to a world in need of hope and affirmation.

BUILDING A FOUNDATION OF SELF RESPECT

There is a cornerstone—the cornerstone of "Building a Foundation of Self-Respect"—in the complex structure of human development and self-esteem. Each of us travels this path as we negotiate the trials and uncertainties of life. It requires inner strength and unchanging self-value. This path is about developing a genuine feeling of self-worth that shines from the inside, not only about getting respect from other people. Imagine the story of Anna, a young woman who had often allowed others to undermine her worth. She found herself in relationships where her boundaries were disregarded, and her self-esteem dwindled. But as she embarked on the path of Building a Foundation of Self-Respect, she discovered the power of setting boundaries, speaking her truth, and valuing herself for who she truly was. Or think of Michael, a man who had faced ridicule and criticism for pursuing his passions. He learned that self-respect meant honoring his dreams and talents, even when they didn't conform to others' expectations.

Building a Foundation of Self-Respect is an act of self-love and self-empowerment. It's about acknowledging your inherent worth as a human being and recognizing that you deserve to be treated with dignity and kindness. It's not about arrogance or entitlement, but about embracing a deep sense of self-value that informs your choices, actions, and interactions with the world. This journey encourages you to set healthy boundaries that safeguard your emotional and mental well-being. It teaches you to assertively communicate your needs and desires, valuing your opinions and feelings even when they differ from others. It prompts you to release the need for external validation and find validation from within, understanding that your worth is not contingent on others' opinions or approval.

Building a Foundation of Self-Respect is a lifelong commitment to self-compassion and self-acceptance. It's a journey that empowers you to stand tall in the face of adversity, embrace your uniqueness, and honor your values and principles. It's a realization that self-respect isn't something to be earned or bestowed upon you; it's something you bestow upon yourself, as a sacred affirmation of your inherent worth. Once you have found strength and liberation it brings self-respect and helps you recognize that, in building this foundation, you not only elevate your well-being but also contribute to a world where respect, kindness, and dignity are cherished values for all.

CHAPTER 6

BREAKING THE CYCLE

There is frequently a pattern in the intricate web of our lives—a pattern that repeats throughout generations, sometimes going unnoticed and other times being painfully clear. We refer to this pattern as "Breaking the Cycle," a path of self-awareness and tenacity that tests us to rise beyond the remnants of the past and forge a better future. Imagine the life of Sarah, a lady who was raised in a dysfunctional family with unresolved issues. She encountered a recurring pattern of toxic relationships and self-destructive actions as she started living as an adult. But she made Breaking the Cycle her life's work out of a desire to rewrite her past and give her kids a supportive atmosphere.

Breaking the Cycle is a quest for change, a dedication to tearing down thought and behavior patterns that no longer serve ourselves or the people we care about. It's a recognition that our history need not determine our present or future and that we can make decisions that promote healing and development. Whether they are poisonous relationships, bad behaviors, or self-limiting beliefs, the patterns we've inherited or perpetuated must be faced during this trip. It challenges us to consider our driving forces, comprehend the causes of our actions, and make active efforts toward a better future.

Breaking the Cycle is not without its challenges, for it often demands courage and resilience. It may require seeking therapy or support, setting firm boundaries, and making tough decisions. It's a journey that involves self-reflection and self-compassion, as we acknowledge that healing is a process, and setbacks are a part of the path.

But in Breaking the Cycle, we discover the profound power of transformation. We learn that we can be the authors of our own stories, and that we can create new patterns of love, connection, and well-being. We recognize that, by breaking destructive cycles, we not only heal ourselves but also pave the way for healthier, more nurturing relationships for future generations.

So, let's embark on this exploration of Breaking the Cycle, let us journey together into the realm of personal growth and healing. Let us celebrate the stories of those who have broken free from the chains of their past and forged new paths of hope and renewal. And let us recognize that, in breaking the cycle, we become agents of positive change, not only for ourselves but for the world around us—a world in need of healing and transformation.

IDENTIFYING NEGATIVE PATTERNS

A thread of unfavorable patterns that might influence our experiences and relationships frequently runs through the intricate tapestry of our lives. The act of becoming aware of these recurrent themes in our lives—patterns that could impede our progress, happiness, and the caliber of our relationships—is known as "identifying negative patterns." Consider the story of Emily, a young woman who found herself repeatedly drawn into relationships that left her feeling unfulfilled and emotionally drained. As she delved into the journey of Identifying Negative Patterns, she noticed common threads in these relationships—patterns of codependency and a tendency to prioritize others' needs over her own. Or think of James, a man whose career aspirations always seemed to end in frustration and disappointment. Through self-reflection, he realized that a fear of success and self-doubt were recurring patterns that held him back.

Identifying Negative Patterns is akin to shining a light into the shadows of our lives, revealing the underlying causes of our recurrent challenges and struggles. It's about recognizing that these patterns are not arbitrary; they often stem from past experiences, childhood conditioning, or unresolved emotional wounds. By identifying them, we gain the power to break free from their grip and make choices that lead to healthier, more fulfilling lives.

This journey encourages us to engage in self-reflection and introspection, to ask ourselves why we find ourselves in familiar, undesirable situations. It prompts us to examine our reactions, behaviors, and thought processes, seeking to uncover the root causes of our patterns. It invites us to seek support and guidance, whether from therapists, mentors, or trusted friends, as we navigate the sometimes-challenging process of self-discovery.

Identifying Negative Patterns is not an act of self-blame but one of self-awareness and empowerment. It's an acknowledgment that we have the capacity to change, to heal, and to create new, positive patterns that serve our well-being and the well-being of those around us. It's a transformative journey that allows us to break free from the shackles of the past and chart a course towards a more fulfilling and authentic life. So, as we explore Identifying Negative Patterns, let's take a voyage into the world of self-awareness and personal development together, dear reader. Let us celebrate the tales of those who were able to identify and break unhealthy habits while gaining strength and insight in the process. Let us remember that by spotting these patterns, we can create good change for not just our own lives but also for the world we live in, a world that desperately needs healing and reform.

CHOOSING DIFFERENT PATHS

We frequently reach a point in the complicated fabric of life where we must stand at a crossroads and make a decision. Choosing Different Paths is a voyage of decision-making and transformation, a turning point where we become aware of our ability to veer off the beaten path and travel down new, unexplored paths. Imagine Alex's experience. Alex spent years pursuing a traditional career path since it was the right thing to do. But when they got to a certain age, they could not help but feel the need to pursue their artistic passions. Choosing Different Paths became their declaration of independence from societal expectations, and they took the courageous step to pursue their true calling. Or think of Sarah, a woman who had long been in a toxic relationship, feeling trapped by her fear of loneliness. Her choice to take a different path was a decision to prioritize self-love and emotional well-being over the comfort of familiarity.

This subtitle Choosing Different Paths is a call to respect our inner voices and desires, even when they go against tradition or accepted social mores. It's about realizing that we have the freedom to redefine our life, take other paths, and look for new opportunities. This trip inspires us to follow our instincts, believe in our intuition, and have the guts to challenge the current quo. Choosing alternative routes frequently requires embracing uncertainty and forging on into the unknown. It might call for letting go of familiar identities, comfort zones, and a sense of adventure. It's a transformational process that encourages us to consider our beliefs, wants, and long-term objectives and pushes us to make decisions that are consistent with our true selves.

This journey isn't about recklessness or impulsivity, but about deliberate and informed decision making. It's about seeking guidance when necessary, learning from past experiences, and being prepared to adapt to the challenges that may arise. It's an affirmation of our capacity for growth and resilience, as we navigate uncharted territories and sculpt our lives in accordance with our true passions and priorities. So, dear reader, as we embark on this exploration of Choosing Different Paths, let us journey together into the realm of self-discovery and courage. Let us celebrate the stories of those who have chosen to rewrite their narratives and embrace the freedom to pursue their authentic dreams. And let us recognize that, in choosing different paths, we not only honor our own unique journeys but also become inspirations for others to follow their hearts and forge their own exceptional paths in this complex tapestry of existence.

THE POWER OF SELF-REFLECTION

In the hustle and bustle of our daily lives, there exists a quiet, transformative force—the force of Self-Reflection. It's a journey into the depths of our thoughts, emotions, and experiences—a journey that requires us to pause, step back, and examine our lives with a discerning eye. This journey, often underestimated in its simplicity, carries immense power to illuminate our path, foster personal growth, and lead us towards a more fulfilling existence. Imagine the story of Rachel, a young woman who had been tirelessly pursuing her career, always on the move, and seemingly climbing the ladder of success. However, she felt an underlying sense of restlessness and disconnectedness. It was only when she began practicing the art of Self-Reflection that she realized she had been neglecting her personal values and passions. Through introspection, she redirected her life towards a path that aligned with her true self.

Self-reflection is an act of awareness and self-compassion. Looking inward and investigating the nuances of our ideas, feelings, and behaviors is a conscious decision. It involves taking the time to get to know ourselves better, identifying our areas of strength and development, and making deliberate choices that promote personal growth. This journey often starts with asking ourselves meaningful questions: What are our goals and values? What motivates us? What fears or insecurities may be holding us back? What patterns of behavior or thought do we want to change? Through this self-inquiry, we gain insight into our desires, fears, and aspirations, and we become better equipped to make choices that align with our authentic selves. The Power of Self-Reflection goes beyond introspection; it extends to personal growth, emotional intelligence, and enhanced decision-making. It allows us to break free from repetitive patterns that no longer serve us, to heal from past wounds, and to cultivate resilience in the face of challenges. It enables us to develop empathy, both towards ourselves and others, fostering healthier relationships and a deeper understanding of human nature.

In a world that often rushes forward, Self-Reflection is the oasis of stillness and mindfulness—a practice that nurtures our inner world and helps us find balance amidst chaos. It's a tool that empowers us to make intentional choices, to appreciate the beauty of the present moment, and to create a life that resonates with our true selves. So, let's take a voyage together into the world of self-discovery and personal development as we explore The Power of Self-Reflection, dear reader. Let's celebrate the success stories of people who have used this transformational energy to get through the challenges of life. And let us remember that when we practice Self-Reflection, we not only improve our own lives but also those around us, a world that is in desperate need of greater self-awareness and mindfulness.

CHAPTER 7

TRUSTING GOD'S TIMING

Ecclesiastes 3:1 Psalm 27:14

There is a thread of divine timing in the fabric of our lives—a power that transcends human impatience and planning. A path of faith, endurance, and surrender, trusting God's timing requires us to let go of our need for control and have faith that there is a bigger picture developing, even when we can't see it clearly. Consider the life of Mark, a man who meticulously created a thorough life plan with deadlines for achieving goals in his job, family, and personal life. However, despite his careful planning, life often took unexpected turns, leaving him feeling frustrated and disappointed. It was only when Mark began to embrace Trusting God's Timing that he found peace and acceptance in the unfolding of his journey, realizing that there was a divine order guiding his steps.

It's important to understand that there are aspects of our lives that are beyond of our control before we can trust God's timing. This doesn't mean we should be passive or do nothing. It's a recognition that a higher wisdom is at work even in the face of obstacles, detours, or delays. This path challenges us to let go of our attachment to certain results and submit to the divine timetable. This submission is an act of strong faith rather than a show of frailty. It's about realizing that the expansive tapestry of existence that the Divine spins may not be visible from our limited vantage point. It acknowledges the fact that the greatest blessings can occasionally take the most unexpected or unexpected shapes.

Trusting God's Timing is an affirmation that the Universe's timeline is not constrained by our human expectations, and it often holds surprises that can enrich our lives beyond measure. This journey also requires patience, a quality that can be challenging to cultivate in a world accustomed to instant gratification. Trusting God's Timing invites us to trust that there is a reason for every season in our lives, and that each moment, whether joyful or challenging, contributes to our growth and spiritual evolution. In the face of uncertainty or adversity, Trusting God's Timing can be a wellspring of hope. It reminds us that, even in the darkest hours, there is a dawn awaiting us. It teaches us to let go of anxiety about the future and to find contentment in the present moment, knowing that we are held in the loving embrace of a divine plan.

So, dear reader, let's take a journey together into the world of faith and patience as we begin this investigation of trusting God's timing. Let's celebrate the success stories of those who discovered peace and meaning by submitting to divine timing. Let's also acknowledge that when we put our faith in God's timing, we not only find comfort in the face of uncertainty but also serve as examples of faith and fortitude to a world that frequently suffers with the unknown and could use more faith in the way life's mysteries play out.

Ecclesiastes 3:1: "To everything there is a season, and a time to every purpose under the heaven."

Psalm 27:14: "Wait on the Lord: be of good courage, and he shall strengthen thine heart: wait, I say, on the Lord."

These verses emphasize the idea that there is a divine timing and purpose for all things and encourage us to patiently wait and trust in the guidance of the Lord.

SURRENDERING CONTROL

Proverbs 3:5-6 Matthew 6:33-34

There is a fundamental and transformational act in the complex dance of life: giving up control. It's a trip that asks us to loosen our hold on life's reins, let go of the idea that we are in charge of shaping our futures, and embrace the beauty of ceding authority to something bigger than ourselves. Think of Lisa, who was fiercely independent and thought she could carefully organize and manage every element of her life. But despite her best efforts, she frequently found herself dealing with unexpected difficulties and setbacks. She did not feel more freedom and calm until she started to practice Surrendering Control.

Surrendering Control is not an act of resignation or weakness; rather, it is an act of profound courage and trust. It's about recognizing the limitations of our human understanding and acknowledging that there are forces and circumstances beyond our influence. This journey encourages us to relinquish our attachment to specific outcomes and to trust that there is a greater plan unfolding, one that we may not fully comprehend. Surrendering Control invites us to confront our fear of the unknown, to release the anxiety that stems from the need to predict and manipulate every aspect of our lives. It's about embracing uncertainty as an inherent part of the human experience and finding serenity in the midst of it. This journey often leads to a deepening of our faith, whether in a higher power, the universe, or the inherent wisdom of life itself.

This process of surrendering is a daily reminder to let go of our ego's need for control and to allow life to unfold gracefully, not as a one-time occurrence. It nudges us to cherish the beauty of the present, to live in the now, and to acknowledge that our wellbeing is not simply reliant on external conditions. Giving up control doesn't mean we become apathetic or complacent in our lives; on the contrary, it gives us the freedom to make decisions based on our inner knowing and intuition. It invites us to align our actions with our values and intentions while releasing the need to micromanage every detail. It teaches us that sometimes the most profound transformations occur when we surrender to the flow of life rather than resisting it.

This exploration of Surrendering Control has brought us into the realm of faith, courage, and inner peace. Let us celebrate the stories of those who have found liberation in surrender. And let us recognize that, in surrendering control, we not only find serenity and freedom but also become beacons of inspiration for a world that often grapples with the illusion of control—a world in need of greater trust and surrender to life's magnificent mysteries.

Proverbs 3:5-6: "Trust in the Lord with all thine heart; and lean not unto thine own understanding. In all thy ways acknowledge him, and he shall direct thy paths."

Matthew 6:33-34: "But seek ye first the kingdom of God, and his righteousness; and all these things shall be added unto you. Take therefore no thought for the morrow: for the morrow shall take thought for the things of itself."

These verses emphasize the importance of trusting in a higher power and seeking divine guidance, rather than relying solely on our own understanding and control. They encourage us to surrender our worries about the future and trust that God will provide and direct our paths.

PATIENCE IN THE WAITING

Psalm 27:14 Isaiah 40:31

There is a place known as Patience in the Waiting in the diverse fabric of our lives that frequently puts our fortitude to the test. Our dreams frequently appear to linger just out of grasp, challenging us to find comfort in the art of waiting. It is a path that needs us to navigate the delicate balance between our wishes and the timing of their realization. Think about Sarah, a woman who desired to start a family but discovered that as the years went by without a kid, she grew craving for motherhood. Or think of John, a recent graduate who aspired to secure his dream job but faced the daunting task of job hunting in a competitive market. Both Sarah and John experienced the inner turmoil of Patience in the Waiting, a journey that taught them profound lessons about resilience and trust.

Becoming patient in the Waiting is not just about passing the time; it's also about developing the art of endurance, the ability to hold onto hope and faith even when things appear hopeless. It's a recognition that the best things in life frequently take time to materialize and that the waiting period itself can be fertile ground for development and change. This trip challenges us to face our desire for rapid gratification and let go of the urge for quick solutions or instantaneous outcomes. It teaches us that having patience is a state of active faith and anticipation rather than being passive. When we face our worries and anxiety about the future and embrace the now, we can find satisfaction and gratitude for what is, which is sometimes a challenge presented by patience in the waiting.

We gain the skill of resilience—the capacity to handle setbacks and disappointments with grace— in the place of Patience in the Waiting. We learn that waiting is an opportunity for preparation and progress rather than a passive state. It exhorts us to make the most of this time by learning new skills, increasing our level of self-awareness, and developing our inner fortitude. Furthermore, Patience in the Waiting enables us to appreciate the wonder of divine timing—the notion that our lives unfold with a rhythm and a purpose. It serves as a reminder that the Universe frequently has plans that are much bigger and wiser than our own, and that waiting could be a crucial component of those plans.

So, dear reader, as we embark on this exploration of Patience in the Waiting, let us journey together into the realm of endurance, hope, and trust. Let us celebrate the stories of those who have discovered strength and wisdom in waiting. And let us recognize that, in practicing patience, we not only find peace amid uncertainty but also become beacons of resilience and faith for a world that often grapples with the art of waiting—a world in need of greater patience and trust in the unfolding of life's mysteries.

Psalm 27:14: "Wait on the Lord: be of good courage, and he shall strengthen thine heart: wait, I say, on the Lord."

Isaiah 40:31: "But they that wait upon the Lord shall renew their strength; they shall mount up with wings as eagles; they shall run, and not be weary; and they shall walk, and not faint."

These verses emphasize the idea of patiently waiting on the Lord, trusting in His timing, and finding renewed strength and courage in the waiting process.

FAITH IN GOD'S PLAN

Jeremiah 29:11 Romans 8:28

Faith in God's Plan is a powerful and transformational force in the vast tapestry of reality. It's a trip that invites us to let go of our need for control, to let go of our worries about the future, and to accept the conviction that a divine purpose is unfolding, even when the road ahead appears to be cloaked in ambiguity. Imagine the experience of Michael, a man who carefully planned out his life's route but then encountered unforeseen turns and circumstances. Michael started to have a strong faith in God's plan as he faced doubt and hardship. He learned that the Universe often weaves together a grander design than our finite minds can conceive, and that sometimes, the most profound blessings emerge from life's most challenging chapters.

Faith in God's Plan is not a passive acceptance of fate; rather, it is a conscious decision to put our faith in a greater power that oversees our life. It's a confirmation that, despite obstacles and disappointments, God has a plan in place that eventually serves our personal development and spiritual advancement. This journey helps us let go of our attachment to certain results and find peace in the knowledge that there is order to the universe, even when we don't fully understand it.

This faith is not blind; it is a belief grounded in the recognition that life's challenges often carry profound lessons. It teaches us that adversity is not a sign of divine abandonment but an opportunity for resilience and transformation. Faith in God's Plan invites us to look beyond immediate circumstances and to see the bigger picture, to trust that our experiences, whether joyful or painful, are threads woven into the rich tapestry of our lives.

In the moments of doubt or despair, Faith in God's Plan is a wellspring of hope. It reminds us that there is a divine intelligence orchestrating the symphony of existence, and that our lives are interconnected with a greater purpose. This faith calls us to cultivate patience and trust that, even when our prayers seem unanswered, there is a divine timing at work—one that may bring blessings beyond our imagination.

Moreover, Faith in God's Plan fosters a sense of gratitude and humility. It encourages us to appreciate the beauty of the present moment, to find contentment in what is, and to recognize the countless ways in which our lives are already blessed. It teaches us to release the burden of constant striving and to rest in the embrace of divine grace. And let us recognize that, in embracing this faith, we not only find peace amidst life's uncertainties but also become beacons of hope and inspiration for a world that often yearns for deeper meaning and connection—a world in need of greater faith in the unfolding of life's divine plan.

Jeremiah 29:11 "For I know the thoughts that I think toward you, saith the Lord, thoughts of peace, and not of evil, to give you an expected end."

Romans 8:28 "And we know that all things work together for good to them that love God, to them who are the called according to his purpose."

These verses affirm the idea that God has a plan for our lives, filled with hope and purpose, and that all experiences, even challenges, ultimately contribute to a greater good according to His divine design.

CHAPTER 8

ROMANS 8:28

In the sacred verses of Romans 8:28, we find a profound and comforting assurance that speaks directly to the human heart. It is a verse that resonates deeply with the essence of faith and trust, offering solace in the face of life's uncertainties and challenges.

"For we know that all things work together for good to them that love God, to them who are the called according to his purpose."

These words remind us that there is a divine orchestration at play in our lives, even when we cannot discern it. They assure us that every experience, whether joyful or painful, is woven into the grand tapestry of our existence, all part of a greater purpose. It's a message that calls upon us to look beyond the surface of our struggles and circumstances and to trust in the benevolence of a higher power.

Romans 8:28 is a ray of hope in difficult circumstances. It inspires us to be consistent in our faith and trust that there is a purpose being fulfilled even in the most difficult circumstances. It serves as a reminder that our difficulties are not random, but rather constituent parts of a bigger picture that help us develop as people and as spiritual beings. This verse is a call to foster trust and patience while letting go of our craving for instant solutions or results. In light of the fact that the divine plan frequently unfolds gradually and subtly, it encourages us to be content in the present. It prompts us to recognize that our lives are interconnected with a greater design, one that encompasses not only our individual well-being but also the well-being of others and the world at large.

Moreover, Romans 8:28 fosters a sense of gratitude and humility. It encourages us to appreciate the blessings that abound in our lives, both seen and unseen. It reminds us that our love for God and our alignment with His purpose can bring forth a profound sense of fulfillment and meaning. Romans 8:28 offers a timeless message of hope and assurance, one that resonates with the human spirit across generations and cultures. It speaks to our innate longing for purpose and meaning, assuring us that, even in life's complexities and challenges, there is a divine plan at work that ultimately leads to our good.

Therefore, when we consider Romans 8:28, dear reader, let us accept its message of faith and trust. Let us take solace in the idea that everything will eventually work out for our benefit. And let us use this assurance as a source of fortitude and fortitude as we travel through the various seasons and uncertainties of life.

THE ROLE OF FAITH IN RELATIONSHIPS

1 Corinthians 13:7 Hebrews 11:1

In the intricate connection of human connections, there is an invisible but essential thread—a thread woven from faith. It's the Role of Faith in Relationships, a force that binds hearts and souls, fostering trust, resilience, and the capacity to weather the storms of life together. Imagine the story of Sarah and David, a couple who navigated the tumultuous waters of a long-distance relationship. They faced the challenges of physical separation and time zone differences, but their unwavering faith in each other and their shared future held them together. Their journey reflects the profound influence of faith in relationships, a force that transcends the barriers of distance and doubt.

Faith in relationships isn't limited to romantic bonds; it extends to friendships, family ties, and the broader network of human connections. It's a belief in the reliability and loyalty of others, a foundation upon which trust is built. This journey encourages us to have faith not only in the people we care about but also in the strength of the connections we share. At its core, the Role of Faith in Relationships involves trust—trust that those we love will be there for us, support us, and honor their commitments. It's the confidence that even in times of adversity or disagreement, the bonds we've forged will remain resilient.

This faith is an affirmation that relationships are worth investing in, worth nurturing, even when challenges arise.

Faith in relationships is not blind; it's a faith rooted in experience and understanding. It's an acknowledgment that relationships aren't immune to difficulties, but it's the belief that together, we can overcome them. This journey often requires open communication, empathy, and the willingness to forgive and move forward. Moreover, the Role of Faith in Relationships encourages us to be vulnerable, to reveal our true selves to others, knowing that we are accepted and loved for who we are. It's a faith that fosters a sense of belonging and connectedness, a belief that we are not alone in our journey through life.

In times of crisis or uncertainty, faith in relationships becomes a source of strength. It's the knowledge that we can lean on each other, share our burdens, and find solace in the support of loved ones. It's a faith that enables us to weather the storms of life with courage and resilience, knowing that we are not alone in facing adversity. Let us journey together into the realm of trust, resilience, and interconnectedness. Let us celebrate the stories of those who have found strength and fulfillment in their connections with others. And let us recognize that, in nurturing faith in our relationships, we not only enrich our lives but also become sources of love, support, and inspiration for a world in need of deeper and more meaningful human connections.

1 Corinthians 13:7 "Beareth all things, believeth all things, hopeth all things, endureth all things."

Hebrews 11:1 "Now faith is the substance of things hoped for, the evidence of things not seen."

These verses highlight the importance of trust, hope, and faith in relationships, underscoring their enduring and transformative nature.

PRAYING FOR CLARITY AND GUIDANCE

Proverbs 3:5-6 James 1:5

Praying for Clarity and Guidance is a powerful and humbling activity that can help you navigate the maze of choices and difficulties in life. It's a path that challenges us to lower our standards, admit the limits of our own knowledge, and turn to heavenly guidance and wisdom when faced with doubt. Think about Emily, a young lady who is faced with a job decision. She was torn between two excellent employment opportunities because they each offered various paths and opportunities. Emily sought direction and clarity through prayer during her periods of uncertainty. She discovered that asking for spiritual direction while making decisions in life is a habit that can bring great insight and peace.

Praying for Clarity and Guidance is an act of surrender, a recognition that there are aspects of our lives that are beyond our control, and that we need divine wisdom to navigate them. It's an affirmation that we are not alone in our journey, that there is a higher power or source of wisdom that we can turn to for counsel. This journey encourages us to cultivate patience, to resist the impulse to rush into decisions, and to create space for reflection and discernment. It prompts us to ask not only for clear answers but also for the wisdom to interpret those answers in the context of our lives.

Moreover, Praying for Clarity and Guidance fosters a sense of trust in the divine plan. It's an acknowledgment that there is a greater purpose and design to our lives, and that even when we cannot see the entire picture, there is a guiding force at work. This trust allows us to release the burden of worry and anxiety, knowing that we are held in the loving embrace of divine wisdom. In times of confusion or adversity, this practice becomes a source of solace. It's a way to find inner peace amidst the chaos of life's uncertainties. It provides a pathway to clarity, allowing us to see through the fog of doubt and fear and make choices that align with our values and intentions.

Praying for Clarity and Guidance isn't confined to major life decisions; it can be applied to everyday choices and challenges as well. It's an ongoing conversation with the divine, a way to seek guidance in both the big and small moments of life. Let's celebrate the stories of those who have found clarity and direction through prayer. And let us recognize that, in seeking divine guidance, we not only find answers to our questions but also deepen our connection to the source of all wisdom—a connection that can illuminate our path through the uncertainties of life.

Proverbs 3:5-6 "Trust in the Lord with all thine heart; and lean not unto thine own understanding.
In all thy ways acknowledge him, and he shall direct thy paths."

James 1:5 "If any of you lack wisdom, let him ask of God, that giveth to all men liberally, and upbraideth not; and it shall be given him."

These verses emphasize the value of trusting in God and seeking His wisdom and guidance in all aspects of life. They encourage us to turn to the divine for direction and clarity in our decisions and challenges.

CULTIVATING A SPIRITUAL CONNECTION

Psalm 46:10 James 4:8

In the midst of life's hustle and bustle, there exists a profound yearning—a yearning to cultivate a Spiritual Connection. It's a journey that beckons us to go beyond the surface of our existence, to seek something deeper, something transcendent that nourishes our souls and brings meaning to our lives. Imagine the story of Daniel, a man who found himself caught in the whirlwind of a demanding career and the pressures of daily life. Yet, in the quiet moments of introspection, he felt a longing for something more, something that would provide solace and purpose. Daniel embarked on the journey of cultivating a Spiritual Connection, and in doing so, he discovered a wellspring of inner peace and wisdom.

Cultivating a Spiritual Connection is not confined to any specific religious practice; it transcends boundaries and embraces the universal essence of spirituality. It's about nurturing a relationship with the divine, the cosmos, or the profound interconnectedness of all things. This journey encourages us to look within, to explore the depths of our own consciousness, and to recognize the presence of something greater than ourselves. At its core, cultivating a Spiritual Connection involves seeking a source of guidance, solace, and inspiration that goes beyond the material realm.
It's an acknowledgment that there is a deeper layer of reality that we can tap into—a realm of inner peace, wisdom, and purpose. This connection often brings a sense of grounding and inner harmony, even in life's storms.

This journey invites us to embrace practices that resonate with our souls, whether it's meditation, prayer, nature walks, or acts of kindness. It encourages us to create moments of stillness in our busy lives, moments where we can tune in to the whispers of our inner selves and the divine presence that surrounds us. Cultivating a Spiritual Connection is about nourishing our spirits, much like tending to a garden. It requires patience, attention, and a willingness to let go of the noise and distractions that often drown out the subtle voice of our inner wisdom. This connection often leads to a greater sense of purpose and compassion, as we recognize our interconnectedness with all living beings.

In moments of solitude and reflection, we often find clarity and answers to life's questions. Cultivating a Spiritual Connection is a pathway to discovering these answers within ourselves, as well as a source of solace during times of uncertainty or grief. We explore the practice of Cultivating a Spiritual Connection, let us journey together into the realm of inner peace, wisdom, and interconnectedness. Let us celebrate the stories of those who have found solace and purpose through their spiritual connections. And let us recognize that, in nurturing this connection, we not only enrich our own lives but also become beacons of light and love in a world that often yearns for deeper meaning and spiritual nourishment—a world in need of profound spiritual connections.

Psalm 46:10 "Be still, and know that I am God: I will be exalted among the heathen, I will be exalted in the earth."

James 4:8 "Draw nigh to God, and he will draw nigh to you. Cleanse your hands, ye sinners; and purify your hearts, ye double-minded."

These verses encourage us to seek moments of stillness and inner reflection to draw closer to the divine and cultivate a deeper spiritual connection.

CHAPTER 9

BUILDING HEALTHY RELATIONSHIPS

Building Healthy Relationships is a key ambition in the complex tapestry of human existence. These ties give us support, company, and a sense of belonging while also forming the threads that make up the fabric of our life. Starting the process of building healthy relationships means starting along a path of development, empathy, and profound connection with other people.

Consider the story of Sarah and Mark, two individuals who met under ordinary circumstances but forged an extraordinary bond. Their relationship was built on a foundation of trust, open communication, and mutual respect. As they navigated the twists and turns of life together, they discovered the key elements that contribute to Building Healthy Relationships.

Building Healthy Relationships is about committing to respecting and appreciating each other for who we are as people. It's about realizing that each of us has a unique set of experiences, viewpoints, and histories and that these differences may bring us together rather than drive us apart. When we welcome variety and treat one another with empathy and respect, healthy relationships flourish. Healthy relationships depend on open communication to survive. It's the art of speaking while also paying close attention to what is being said. We discover the value of active listening and the need to seek understanding before seeking it to create and maintain meaningful connections. Establishing trust, resolving problems, and establishing emotional ties all result from effective communication.

Every healthy relationship is built on trust. It's the assurance that we can count on one another and that our words and deeds are reliable and consistent. While trust must be earned over time, it may be lost in an instant. It is a delicate but crucial component that forms the basis of relationships that last. To create healthy relationships, boundaries are essential. They outline the boundary between taking care of oneself and taking care of others, ensuring that our needs and limitations are honored. Open discussions regarding boundaries are a sign of healthy relationships because they help us strike the right balance between giving and receiving without feeling resentful or overworked.

Forgiveness is the salve that heals the wounds of miscommunication or hurtful actions. In any relationship, there are moments of friction and misunderstanding. A willingness to forgive and seek resolution is a hallmark of a healthy connection. It allows us to move forward with grace and understanding. Empathy is the ability to step into another's shoes, to feel what they feel, and to respond with compassion. It's the bridge that connects hearts in times of joy and sorrow. In Building Healthy Relationships, we cultivate empathy to deepen our connections and offer genuine support.

Ultimately, Building Healthy Relationships is an ongoing journey, a commitment to nurturing the connections that matter most in our lives. It requires effort, patience, and a willingness to grow as individuals and as partners or friends. These relationships are not without their challenges, but they offer a wellspring of love, companionship, and shared experiences that enrich the tapestry of our lives.

Proverbs 17:17 "A friend loveth at all times, and a brother is born for adversity."

1 Corinthians 13:4-7 "Charity suffereth long, and is kind; charity envieth not; charity vaunteth not itself, is not puffed up, doth not behave itself unseemly, seeketh not her own, is not easily provoked, thinketh no evil; rejoiceth not in iniquity, but rejoiceth in the truth; beareth all things, believeth all things, hopeth all things, endureth all things."

These verses emphasize the importance of love, kindness, and enduring support in building and maintaining healthy relationships. They provide guidance on how to cultivate meaningful connections with others.

SETTING BOUNDARIES

In the intricate dance of human interactions, there is a crucial element—Setting Boundaries. It's a vital act of self-care and self-respect, a practice that fosters healthy relationships and personal well-being. To embark on the journey of Setting Boundaries is to embrace a crucial aspect of human connections, one that allows us to navigate the delicate balance between giving and preserving our own needs and limits. Imagine the story of Alex, a kind-hearted individual who often found himself overwhelmed by the demands and expectations of others. He would go to great lengths to accommodate everyone's wishes, even at the expense of his own time and wellbeing. It was only when Alex began Setting Boundaries that he discovered the transformative power of this practice.

At its core, Setting Boundaries involves defining the limits of what is acceptable and respectful in our interactions with others. It's an act of communicating our needs, expectations, and personal space clearly and assertively. Healthy boundaries help us protect our physical and emotional wellbeing, maintain our autonomy, and preserve our values and priorities. Boundary-setting is not a rejection of others; rather, it's a recognition that our needs and limitations deserve respect just as much as anyone else's. It's an affirmation that we are responsible for our own happiness and wellbeing, and that we have the right to say "no" when necessary. Healthy boundaries serve as a protective shield against manipulation, exploitation, or emotional exhaustion.

Effective communication is a crucial aspect of Setting Boundaries. It's about expressing our needs and limits with clarity, empathy, and respect. Healthy boundary-setting involves open and honest conversations, where we assertively communicate our boundaries while acknowledging the needs and feelings of others. It's a skill that allows us to navigate relationships with authenticity and mutual understanding. In personal relationships, Setting Boundaries can enhance intimacy and respect. It allows us to express our desires and expectations, fostering deeper connections based on consent and mutual agreement. It also helps us navigate conflicts constructively, as boundaries provide a framework for resolving disagreements while respecting each person's rights and limits.

Boundary-setting isn't limited to personal relationships; it extends to professional and social settings as well. In the workplace, healthy boundaries help prevent burnout and promote work-life balance. In social situations, they allow us to choose how we spend our time and energy, ensuring that our own well-being remains a priority. Setting Boundaries is a powerful act of selfcare and self-respect. It's a practice that fosters healthy relationships, bolsters our emotional resilience, and empowers us to lead more authentic and fulfilling lives. It's an acknowledgment that we are responsible for defining and preserving the sanctity of our own space, both physical and emotional. And it's a journey toward greater personal empowerment and well-being, where we learn to prioritize ourselves without guilt or apology.

Proverbs 25:28 "He that hath no rule over his own spirit is like a city that is broken down, and without walls."

2 Corinthians 6:14 "Be ye not unequally yoked together with unbelievers: for what fellowship hath righteousness with unrighteousness? and what communion hath light with darkness?"

These verses emphasize the importance of self-control and discernment in relationships, highlighting the value of maintaining boundaries to protect one's well-being and values.

EFFECTIVE COMMUNICATION

In the intricate web of human connections, there is a vital element that serves as the lifeblood of all meaningful interactions—Effective Communication. It's a skill and an art, a practice that transcends words alone. To embark on the journey of Effective Communication is to embark on a path of understanding, connection, and the profound ability to convey our thoughts, feelings, and intentions with clarity and empathy. Consider the story of Emma and James, a couple who navigated the peaks and valleys of their relationship with the powerful tool of Effective Communication. Through open and honest dialogue, they learned to understand each other's needs and perspectives, transforming conflicts into opportunities for growth and connection.

At its core, Effective Communication is about more than just speaking; it's about listening deeply and attentively. It's the act of not only conveying our thoughts and feelings but also seeking to truly understand those of others. This journey teaches us to engage in conversations with empathy and the genuine intention to connect. Clarity is a cornerstone of Effective Communication. It's about expressing ourselves in a way that is easily understood by others. It involves using plain and simple language, avoiding jargon or ambiguity that might hinder comprehension. When we communicate clearly, we bridge gaps and foster mutual understanding.

Active listening is a practice within Effective Communication that involves not only hearing words but also tuning in to the emotions and unspoken messages behind them. It requires patience, the ability to remain present, and the willingness to set aside our own judgments and assumptions to fully grasp the perspectives of others.

Empathy is a powerful aspect of Effective Communication. It's the capacity to step into another person's shoes, to feel what they feel, and to respond with compassion. When we communicate empathetically, we create an environment where others feel heard, valued, and understood, strengthening the bonds of trust and connection.

Conflict resolution is another facet of Effective Communication. It's the skill of addressing disagreements or misunderstandings in a constructive and respectful manner. Instead of avoiding conflicts or escalating them, this practice allows us to find common ground and seek mutually beneficial solutions.

Non-verbal communication, such as body language and facial expressions, plays a significant role in Effective Communication. These subtle cues can convey emotions and intentions that words alone may not express. Learning to interpret and use non-verbal cues enhances our ability to communicate authentically and connect with others on a deeper level.

In both personal and professional relationships, Effective Communication is a catalyst for building trust, resolving conflicts, and nurturing meaningful connections. It allows us to express our needs and desires, share our joys and sorrows, and create a shared understanding of the world with those around us.

So, dear reader, as we delve into the practice of Effective Communication, let us journey together into the realm of understanding, connection, and empathy. Let us celebrate the stories of those who have learned the art of communicating effectively and the transformations it has brought to their lives. And let us recognize that, in mastering this skill, we not only enrich our own relationships but also contribute to a world that thrives on clear, empathetic, and authentic communication—a world where connections flourish, misunderstandings diminish, and understanding prevails.

Proverbs 18:13: "He that answereth a matter before he heareth it, it is folly and shame unto him."

James 1:19: "Wherefore, my beloved brethren, let every man be swift to hear, slow to speak, slow to wrath."

These verses emphasize the value of listening attentively and speaking thoughtfully, key components of effective communication. They encourage us to approach conversations with patience and understanding.

GROWING TOGETHER IN CHRIST

The desire to grow together in Christ is a fundamental yearning that believers share as they travel through life. It is a spiritual journey that crosses all geographical boundaries and unites people in their shared love for Christ, faith, and purpose. Starting down the path of Growing Together in Christ is starting a journey of deep spiritual connection, support, and nutrition with other believers. Imagine the tale of Sarah and David, two people from quite different backgrounds who were brought together by their mutual faith in Jesus. Their bond was founded not only on shared passions but also on a shared love of God. Through their shared spiritual journey, they discovered the transformative power of Growing Together in Christ.

At its core, Growing Together in Christ involves nurturing and deepening our relationship with God alongside fellow believers. It's about recognizing that our faith isn't a solitary endeavor but a shared experience. It encourages us to support one another in our spiritual growth, to uplift each other in prayer, and to hold one another accountable in our Christian walk. Unity in Christ is a central theme of Growing Together in Christ. It's the acknowledgment that, regardless of our differences, we are bound by the unifying love of Jesus Christ. This unity transcends denominational or theological distinctions, inviting believers from all walks of life to come together in worship, fellowship, and service.

Prayer becomes the heartbeat of Growing Together in Christ. It's the conduit through which believers communicate with God and intercede for one another. When we pray together, we share our joys, sorrows, and spiritual needs, deepening our bond with God and each other. Studying the Scriptures as a community is another integral aspect of this journey. It allows believers to explore and apply the teachings of Christ together, fostering spiritual growth, understanding, and wisdom. Bible studies, discussions, and reflections become opportunities to learn from one another's perspectives and experiences.

Accountability within the community is vital. Believers hold each other to high moral and ethical standards, ensuring that their actions align with their faith. This accountability encourages spiritual growth and transformation, as individuals strive to live out the teachings of Christ in their daily lives. Worship and praise are the shared expressions of gratitude and devotion in Growing Together in Christ. Gatherings for worship, whether in churches, small groups, or fellowship events, provide opportunities for believers to collectively lift their voices and hearts to God, deepening their connection with Him and one another.

Service to others is a natural outflow of this journey. Believers are inspired to serve their communities and the world, driven by the love of Christ. Growing Together in Christ fosters a spirit of compassion and a commitment to making a positive impact in the lives of others.

Growing Together in Christ is a journey of spiritual enrichment, unity, and profound connection. It's a recognition that faith is not meant to be a solitary pursuit but a shared experience that enriches our lives and the lives of those around us. Through this journey, believers find strength, support, and a deeper sense of purpose as they grow together in their love for Christ and their love for one another.

Hebrews 10:24-25 "And let us consider one another to provoke unto love and to good works: Not forsaking the assembling of ourselves together, as the manner of some is; but exhorting one another: and so much the more, as ye see the day approaching."

1 Corinthians 1:10

"Now I beseech you, brethren, by the name of our Lord Jesus Christ, that ye all speak the same thing, and that there be no divisions among you; but that ye be perfectly joined together in the same mind and in the same judgment."

These verses underscore the importance of gathering as believers to support and encourage one another in their faith journey, promoting unity and love within the community of Christ.

CHAPTER 10

EMBRACING YOUR SINGLENESS

In the diverse tapestry of life, there's an often overlooked but profound chapter—the chapter of Embracing Your Singleness. It's a time when an individual finds themselves walking a path that is uniquely their own, a time to cultivate self-discovery, personal growth, and the freedom to chart one's course. To embrace singleness is to embark on a journey of self-love, empowerment, and a deep appreciation for the beauty of solo exploration. Imagine the story of Emily, a vibrant and independent woman who found herself single after a long-term relationship ended. Instead of viewing this as a setback, she saw it as an opportunity—a chance to rediscover herself, her passions, and her aspirations. Emily embarked on a journey of Embracing Her Singleness, and it transformed her life in ways she never imagined.

At its core, Embracing Your Singleness is not about seeking solitude but about celebrating the unique chapter of life when one is unburdened by romantic commitments. It's about recognizing the inherent value in being single, a state that provides the space and freedom to explore one's interests, values, and goals. Singleness becomes a time for self-discovery, personal growth, and self-love. Self-love is a central theme in this journey. It's the practice of cherishing and nurturing oneself, free from the influence of external relationships. When one learns to love themselves deeply, they discover that they are complete and whole as an individual, regardless of their relationship status. This self-love is the foundation upon which a fulfilling and healthy future relationship can be built.

Personal growth is another pivotal aspect of Embracing Your Singleness. It's the opportunity to invest time and energy in one's own development, whether through education, hobbies, travel, or self-improvement. The freedom that singleness affords allows for personal exploration and the pursuit of dreams and passions. Independence becomes a cherished gift during this phase of life.
It's the ability to make decisions without the constraints of a partner's desires or expectations. Independence fosters self-reliance, resilience, and the capacity to face life's challenges with confidence.

Friendships take on a special significance in the journey of Embracing Your Singleness. These bonds become sources of support, laughter, and companionship. Friendships offer the opportunity to create a chosen family, a network of people who uplift and stand by your side.

Community involvement and social engagement can also flourish during this period. As one becomes more comfortable with their singleness, they often seek out opportunities to give back to the community, participate in social activities, and make meaningful connections with others.

Embracing Your Singleness is not about closing the door to future relationships but about opening it with a sense of completeness and self-assuredness. It's about being selective and waiting for a relationship that complements and enhances one's life, rather than relying on it to complete it. Embracing Your Singleness is a journey of self-love, self-discovery, and personal empowerment. It's a chapter that offers the freedom to explore, grow, and cultivate a deep sense of contentment as an individual. It's an acknowledgment that being single is not a state of lack but a beautiful opportunity for personal flourishing and fulfillment—a time to embrace the unique and remarkable individual that you are.

1Corinthians 7:32-34 "But I would have you without carefulness. He that is unmarried careth for the things that belong to the Lord, how he may please the Lord: But he that is married careth for the things that are of the world, how he may please his wife. There is difference also between a wife and a virgin. The unmarried woman careth for the things of the Lord, that she may be holy both in body and in spirit: but she that is married careth for the things of the world, how she may please her husband."

Psalm 46:10 "Be still, and know that I am God: I will be exalted among the heathen, I will be exalted in the earth."

These verses emphasize the benefits of singleness, including the ability to focus on one's relationship with God and to lead a life that is less encumbered by worldly concerns. They suggest that singleness can be a time for spiritual growth and devotion.

THE BEAUTY OF SINGLENESS

In the grand tapestry of life, there exists a unique and often underappreciated thread—the thread of Singleness. It's a chapter in life when an individual walks a path that is uniquely their own, a time of profound self-discovery, personal growth, and the freedom to fully embrace their own identity. To recognize the Beauty of Singleness is to embark on a journey of self-empowerment, self-love, and the profound appreciation of the value of solitude. Consider the story of Michael, a thoughtful and independent man who, despite societal expectations, reveled in his single status. Michael didn't view his singleness as a void to be filled but as an opportunity—a chance to immerse himself in self-discovery, nurture his passions, and become the best version of himself. Through this journey, he unearthed the Beauty of Singleness.

At its core, the Beauty of Singleness is rooted in the understanding that being single is not a deficiency to be remedied by a relationship but a unique season of life to be celebrated. It's about recognizing that one's self-worth and happiness are not contingent on having a partner. Singleness is a time of liberation, a period when individuals can cultivate a deep sense of self-love and appreciation for their own identity.

Self-love is the heart of this journey. It's the practice of cherishing and nurturing oneself, free from the influence of external relationships. When one learns to love themselves deeply, they discover that they are complete and whole as an individual, regardless of their relationship status. Self-love is the foundation upon which a fulfilling and healthy future relationship can be built, as it sets a standard for how one should be treated and respected. Personal growth flourishes during this phase of life. It's the opportunity to invest time and energy in one's own development, whether through education, hobbies, travel, or self-improvement. The freedom that singleness affords allows for personal exploration and the pursuit of dreams and passions. It's a chance to build a life that aligns with one's aspirations and values.

Independence becomes a cherished gift during this journey. It's the ability to make decisions without the constraints of a partner's desires or expectations. Independence fosters self-reliance, resilience, and the capacity to face life's challenges with confidence. It empowers individuals to define their own path and forge their unique destiny.

Friendships take on a special significance in the Beauty of Singleness. These connections become sources of support, laughter, and companionship. Friendships offer the opportunity to create a chosen family, a network of people who uplift and stand by your side. They provide a rich tapestry of human connection and emotional support.

Community involvement and social engagement can also flourish during this period. As one becomes more comfortable with their singleness, they often seek out opportunities to give back to the community, participate in social activities, and make meaningful connections with others. Singleness can offer the freedom to invest time in social causes and create a positive impact in the world. The Beauty of Singleness is a journey of self-love, self-discovery, and personal empowerment. It's a chapter that offers the freedom to explore, grow, and cultivate a deep sense of contentment as an individual. It's an acknowledgment that being single is not a state of lack but a beautiful opportunity for personal flourishing and fulfillment—a time to embrace the unique and remarkable individual that you are.

1 Corinthians 7:32-34: "But I would have you without carefulness. He that is unmarried careth for the things that belong to the Lord, how he may please the Lord: But he

that is married careth for the things that are of the world, how he may please his wife. There is also a difference between a wife and a virgin. The unmarried woman careth for the things of the Lord, that she may be holy both in body and in spirit: but she that is married careth for the things of the world, how she may please her husband."

Psalm 46:10: "Be still, and know that I am God: I will be exalted among the heathen, I will be exalted in the earth."

These verses highlight the value of singleness as a time to focus on one's relationship with God, personal growth, and the pursuit of holiness. They encourage individuals to find contentment and peace in their current state, knowing that it allows for a deeper connection with God.

SERVING GOD WHOLEHEARTEDLY

There is a profound calling that exists in the path of faith and spirituality—the calling to Serve God Wholeheartedly. It serves as an invitation to commit one's life, abilities, and deeds to a greater good and to set out on a path where each step is performed with unflinching devotion and a powerful sense of purpose. Serving God fully entails making a lifetime commitment and embarking on a spiritual journey that penetrates one's very nature, going beyond rituals and traditions. Imagine the story of Sarah, a woman whose life was transformed when she embraced the call to Serve God Wholeheartedly. It was not a decision born out of obligation, but a heartfelt response to a divine encounter that ignited a fire within her. Sarah's journey was marked by an unshakable faith, selfless love, and an unwavering desire to make a meaningful impact on the world around her.

Serving God Wholeheartedly is about coordinating one's life with divine purpose. It's a recognition that our life goes beyond the ordinary and that we are a part of a larger story that the Divine has penned. This experience motivates us to live deliberately and pursue the higher purpose that speaks to our souls. Selflessness and selfless love are components of wholehearted service. It is the readiness to prioritize others' wants and worries over our own. It involves acting with compassion, love, and humility to emulate Jesus Christ, who set an example by humbling Himself to serve others.

The foundation of this journey is prayer. It's how we communicate with God, asking for direction, fortitude, and discernment of His will. We express our appreciation, convey our concerns, and wishes, and ask God's presence in every area of our life through prayer. Our interactions with other people are also a part of our wholehearted service. It's about showing others around us how much God loves them and being a source of inspiration, comfort, and hope for them. It entails cultivating empathy, compassion, and forgiveness while acknowledging the divine spark present in every person.

Living a life of wholehearted service often leads to acts of kindness and generosity. It's about being attuned to the needs of the less fortunate and taking action to alleviate their suffering. It's about sharing our blessings, whether material or spiritual, with a spirit of abundance and gratitude. This journey calls us to embrace our unique gifts and talents as instruments of service.

It encourages us to use our abilities to bring about positive change in the world, whether through teaching, healing, creating art, or any other form of expression that glorifies God.

Resilience is a hallmark of Serving God Wholeheartedly. It acknowledges that life's journey is not without challenges, but it equips us with the spiritual fortitude to persevere in the face of adversity. It reminds us that, even in our moments of weakness, God's grace is sufficient. Serving God Wholeheartedly is not a task to be completed but a lifelong commitment. It's a journey that encompasses the entirety of our being—our thoughts, actions, and intentions. It's an unwavering dedication to living a life that reflects the love, grace, and purpose of our Creator. It's an invitation to embrace the profound joy and fulfillment that come from aligning our lives with the divine calling to serve wholeheartedly.

Joshua 24:15 "And if it seem evil unto you to serve the LORD, choose you this day whom ye will serve; whether the gods which your fathers served that were on the other side of the flood, or the gods of the Amorites, in whose land ye dwell: but as for me and my house, we will serve the
LORD."

Colossians 3:23-24 "And whatsoever ye do, do it heartily, as to the Lord, and not unto men;
Knowing that of the Lord ye shall receive the reward of the inheritance: for ye serve the Lord Christ."

These verses emphasize the wholehearted commitment to serving the Lord and doing all things as if we are doing them for Him. They inspire us to prioritize God's will and purpose in our lives and to serve with dedication and devotion.

PREPARING FOR THE RIGHT ONE

The quest for the right person in our lives often takes us on a journey of self-discovery and personal development. Why is it that many struggle to find and keep the right person? The answer often lies in our own preparedness, in our ability to become the right person ourselves. It's a journey that goes beyond appearances and initial attraction; it's about cultivating the qualities that make us not only attractive to others but capable of sustaining a healthy and loving relationship.

Picture Sarah, a woman who found herself repeatedly facing the challenge of attracting the right partner. It wasn't until she took a step back to work on herself that she discovered the key to a lasting and meaningful relationship. Sarah realized that preparing for the right one meant focusing on self-improvement and personal growth. At its core, preparing for the right one begins with self-awareness. It's about taking a close look at our character, our values, and our actions. Are we the kind of person we would want to be with? Are we kind, compassionate, and understanding? Self-awareness is the first step towards identifying areas where we can improve ourselves.

Developing good character is a crucial aspect of this journey. It involves qualities like integrity, honesty, and kindness. These attributes not only make us better individuals but also create a solid foundation for a healthy relationship. When we possess good character, we become trustworthy and reliable partners.

Communication skills are another essential component. Effective communication is the bridge that connects hearts and minds. It's about listening attentively, expressing ourselves clearly, and being open to understanding our partner's perspective. When we communicate well, we foster a deeper connection and avoid misunderstandings.

Hospitality and warmth play a role in making us more inviting to others. These qualities create an atmosphere of comfort and acceptance. When we are hospitable and warm, we make those around us feel valued and appreciated, laying the groundwork for strong and loving relationships.

Love and care are the cornerstones of any lasting partnership. Preparing for the right one involves cultivating a deep sense of love and care not only for ourselves but also for others. Love is the force that binds two people together, and genuine care ensures that we nurture and support our partner in their journey.

Letting go of self-consciousness is crucial. It's easy to get caught up in worrying about how we appear to others. However, when we are comfortable with ourselves, we become more authentic and open in our interactions. True connection happens when we can be ourselves without fear of judgment.

Ultimately, preparing for the right one is about becoming the best version of ourselves, not for someone else, but for our own growth and fulfillment. It's a journey that requires self-reflection, effort, and dedication. It's about recognizing that the right person will be drawn to the qualities we have cultivated within ourselves. It's a journey that not only leads us to the right one but also to a deeper understanding of who we are and what we have to offer in a loving and fulfilling relationship.

"Keep thy heart with all diligence; for out of it are the issues of life."

Ephesians 4:2-3: "With all lowliness and meekness, with longsuffering, forbearing one another in love; Endeavouring to keep the unity of the Spirit in the bond of peace."

These verses highlight the significance of guarding one's heart and cultivating qualities such as humility, patience, and love in preparation for meaningful relationships. They emphasize the importance of personal growth and character development in building strong and harmonious connections with others.

CONCLUSION

BREAKING FREE FROM DENIAL

In the grand narrative of our lives, there comes a pivotal moment—an awakening, a realization that shakes the very foundations of our existence. It's the moment we confront our own denial and take the courageous step towards Breaking Free from Denial. This journey is one of liberation, self-discovery, and the pursuit of a life lived in truth and authenticity.

Imagine the story of Alex, who had spent years in denial, clinging to a version of reality that shielded them from uncomfortable truths. It wasn't until a profound moment of self-reflection that Alex realized the cost of denial—a life half-lived, relationships built on falsehoods, and a deep-seated inner turmoil. With determination, they embarked on the journey to Break Free from Denial, a journey that would transform their life in unimaginable ways.

At its core, Breaking Free from Denial is about the courage to face our own truths, no matter how uncomfortable they may be. It's an acknowledgment that denial keeps us imprisoned in a false narrative, preventing us from living authentically and fully. This journey challenges us to confront our fears, insecurities, and self-deceptions head-on. Self-awareness becomes our guiding light. It's the mirror we hold up to our own souls, reflecting our strengths, weaknesses, and vulnerabilities. Self-awareness is the compass that helps us navigate the treacherous waters of denial, guiding us towards a place of clarity and self-acceptance.

Acceptance is the cornerstone of this journey. It's the willingness to acknowledge our mistakes, limitations, and imperfections. It's also the capacity to accept others for who they are, free from the filters of denial. Acceptance liberates us from the need to control and manipulate our own narrative, allowing us to embrace the full spectrum of human experiences. Healing is an integral part of Breaking Free from Denial. It's the process of mending the wounds that denial has caused: wounds in ourselves and in our relationships. Healing involves forgiveness, not only of others but also of ourselves. It's about letting go of the past and opening ourselves to a future unburdened by denial's chains.

Authenticity becomes our guiding star. It's the commitment to living in alignment with our true selves. Authenticity requires vulnerability, the willingness to be seen and known as we truly are. It's a path that leads to genuine connections with others, built on trust and mutual understanding. Empowerment is the reward of Breaking Free from Denial. It's the newfound strength that comes from living in truth and authenticity. It's the ability to make choices that align with our values and aspirations, rather than being driven by fear or denial. Empowerment allows us to rewrite our own narrative and shape our destiny.

In conclusion, Breaking Free from Denial is not a journey for the faint of heart. It's a journey that demands courage, introspection, and a deep commitment to the truth. It's a journey that liberates us from the confines of denial, allowing us to step into the fullness of our humanity. It's a journey that leads to a life of greater fulfillment, authenticity, and connection with ourselves and the world around us.

Made in the USA
Middletown, DE
07 January 2024